A BRIEF HISTORY *of*

SAFETY HARBOR
❧ FLORIDA ❧

WARREN FIRSCHEIN AND LAURA KEPNER

THE
History
PRESS

Published by The History Press
Charleston, SC 29403
www.historypress.net

Front cover, top: Terrie Thomas. *Bottom*: Heritage Village Archives and Library.

Back cover, top: Safety Harbor Museum and Cultural Center. *Bottom*: Terrie Thomas.

First published 2013

ISBN 9781540208774

Library of Congress CIP data applied for.

"Where Healing Waters Flow™" is a registered trademark of Safety Harbor Resort and Spa. Used with permission.

For the mound builders and those who gave us mystery and a legacy of wonder.

For the citrus growers, railroad workers, protectors, laborers, lawmakers and builders.

*For each generation of children who ran barefoot, climbed high oaks, rode bikes
down Main and swam in the bay.*

For the women who never gave up on a library.

For the ones who weren't remembered because no one ever wrote their stories;

and for the ones whose stories we do have—upon which we have all depended.

For those who are here today, who realize that we are all fortunate

to know one another and to know this city,

and for the people stretched far into time, who will become Safety Harbor's future.

CONTENTS

Acknowledgements   7
Chronology of Events   11
Introduction   15

PART I. BEFORE THE FIRST SETTLERS
1. Was He or Wasn't He?: The Enduring Myth of Hernando de Soto
   and the Espiritu Santo Springs   21
2. The Tragic End of Fray Luis Cancer de Barbastro   28
3. Pedro Menéndez de Avilés and the Calusa-Tocobaga Peace Treaty   33
4. The Tocobaga People of Safety Harbor   40

PART II. THE PIONEERS AND EARLY SETTLERS OF GREEN SPRINGS
5. Odet Philippe: The First Pioneer   55
6. Philippe's Legacy: Safety Harbor's Impact on the Citrus Industry   63
7. The Early Pioneers, 1842–1885   68
8. The Espiritu Santo Springs   78
9. The Development of the Community of Green Springs, 1885–1917   88

PART III. THE COMMUNITY OF SAFETY HARBOR: FROM 1917 TO TODAY
10. Devastation and Growth of a New City   99
11. The History and Development of the Safety Harbor Spa   111
12. The Railroad   121
13. Safety Harbor's Black Community: A Hidden History   127

CONTENTS

14. From World War II to the End of the Millennium:
    The Changing Community   138
15. Civic Organizations: Safety Harbor's Police Department,
    Fire Department and More   149
16. Today's Safety Harbor   160

Appendix 1. Mayors of the City of Safety Harbor   169
Appendix 2. List of Postmasters of the City of Safety Harbor 171
Appendix 3. Approximate Annual Festival Schedule   173
Bibliography   175
Index   187
About the Authors   192

ACKNOWLEDGEMENTS

T he effort of putting together this book involved the assistance of a large number of talented and dedicated people, without whose help this project might never have been completed.

We owe a great debt of gratitude to the board and staff of the Safety Harbor Museum and Cultural Center, especially its curator, Scott Anderson, who provided invaluable information about the early city history, as well as vintage photographs from its exhibits and archives.

The librarians and staff at the Safety Harbor Public Library were always ready and willing to assist us with our research and provided access to their collection of early issues of the *Safety Harbor Herald* as it was in the process of being digitized. Special thanks to Lisa Kothe, Gina Bingham and Mallory Cyr for their help, as well as for their enthusiasm regarding this project. Wes Elliott nimbly obtained dozens of volumes from other library systems nationwide, and we didn't lose a single one.

Matt Spoor, the Safety Harbor city manager, was our "go-to" guy whenever we needed a particular piece of information, and he never failed to connect us with the right source. Mayor Joe Ayoub provided us with encouragement. Bobbie Wheeler directed us to Donna Mack, who guided us in our African American history research, for which we are extremely thankful. Janene McCulley provided us with a listing of the city's mayors, Postmaster Brian Strasser gave us a list of each of Safety Harbor's postmasters and Ray Duke provided information about the history of the fire department. The Safety Harbor Chamber of Commerce identified residents for us to interview.

Shannon Schafer and Katie Bishop assisted us as well. Jean Barraclough, the executive administrator at the Safety Harbor Resort and Spa, provided us with some history of that facility.

Heritage Village, located in Largo, Florida, is a twenty-one-acre park containing over two dozen historic structures, including the log cabin built by James P. "Captain Jim" McMullen and the original Safety Harbor Methodist Episcopal Church. We are grateful for the use of its archives and to volunteer Ernst Upmeyer for his unfailing assistance in helping us identify and locate photographs pertaining to Safety Harbor's early history.

Many longtime residents of the city were kind enough to share their memories and experiences with us, in some cases spending hours describing what it was like to grow up and/or live here in different eras. These include, in alphabetical order: Goldie Banks, William Blackshear, Sandie Brasfield, Caryl Dennis, Laura Dent, Sus Devnani, Pastor Ginny Ellis and many delightful members of the Safety Harbor Presbyterian Church, Yvonne Hedgeman, Mavis Herring, Kim Lashington, B.J. Lehman, Jewel McKeon, Bobby Morrow, Luella Myrick, David Nichols, Valerie Petree Nolte, Christine Petellat, Clyde Rigsby, Joe Samnik, Lois Spencer, Judi Baker Steffens, Dolly Brader Whitehead and all the members of the "I Grew Up in Safety Harbor" Facebook group, who are too numerous to identify individually. You all truly epitomize Safety Harbor's spirit of community, and we are honored to have had the opportunity to meet each and every one of you. Thank you.

A number of people unrelated to the city of Safety Harbor shared their expertise with us and deserve special recognition. Local historian Jim Schnur provided encouragement and support, and we relied heavily on his detailed written materials about the early settlers of Pinellas County, particularly the biography of James P. "Captain Jim" McMullen. In response to an innocuous question, Professor Jerald T. Milanich e-mailed us from Bratislava, Slovakia, to correct a widely circulated misconception about the Tocobaga and pointed us in the right direction. Dr. Michael Francis enthusiastically provided context to the early Spanish expeditions, especially with regard to the origin of the Fountain of Youth myth. Christopher Fowler of the Florida Department of State's Bureau of Historic Preservation helped us navigate through the process of obtaining copies of the state's archaeology files pertaining to excavations and surveys within Safety Harbor. Tom Pavluvcik provided us with his materials about the history of the railroad through Pinellas County and kindly reviewed an early draft of that chapter for accuracy. Gerald Bagwell of the Fort Lauderdale Fire and Safety Museum shared his knowledge of early fire trucks when our search for Safety Harbor's original American LaFrance hit a dead end. Patrick Barnum helped uncover an obscure connection between the McMullen family and P.T. Barnum, which (unfortunately) didn't make it into the final draft but deserves mention for his efforts.

Several talented artists and photographers were kind enough to share their work with us and permit us to reproduce it in these pages for nothing more than our thanks. Stuart Dwork and Theodore Morris each allowed us to use their artwork depicting the Tocobaga. Jon Houglum gave us permission to include his portrait of Odet Philippe, which hangs in the Safety Harbor Museum and Cultural Center. The superbly talented Terrie Thomas, Holly Apperson and Marcia Biggs offered use of their photographs depicting today's Safety Harbor. The Pinellas County Communications Department allowed us to reprint its beautiful photo of the McMullen log cabin, which is available from the website of Heritage Village. Ari Kepner expertly drew the beautiful map that appears in the introduction. Ari also helped with the tedious task of combing through old issues of the *Safety Harbor Herald* in a back room of the library.

Dawn Goldsmith provided much-needed editorial support and technical help with scanning images after we proved time and again that we lacked the skills to do it ourselves. Barbara Finkelstein, too, offered her always-insightful comments on the completed manuscript and led us on a field trip through Philippe Park to show us the location of several remaining citrus trees. Jeff Rosenfield helped promote the project on the *Safety Harbor Patch*. Janet Lee Stinson memorialized the effort to research and produce this work with a remarkable video. Artists Todd Ramquist and Kiaralinda provided continuous encouragement. Craig Davide of Nolan's Pub always gave us a table to discuss the progress of the project. Mike and Joan Kelly also had a table waiting at the 8th Avenue Pub for times whenever we needed a place to negotiate ideas.

Above all, we are grateful to the members of the Safety Harbor Writers & Poets group for their indispensable editorial advice and for providing us with a forum to explore our words and ideas. These include: Amy, Barbara, Deb, Janet Lee, John, Luke, N.B., Nicole, Romeo and Stuart, as well as others who periodically dropped in. You are an immensely talented group of writers and continually pushed us to improve this manuscript in a multitude of ways.

We also wish to send a sincere note of thanks to our editors Chad Rhoad and Jaime Muehl. We are grateful to them and the team at The History Press for believing in us as writers and for including us in such an important endeavor.

ACKNOWLEDGEMENTS

In addition to those above, our families helped make this book a reality through their support and encouragement throughout the entirety of the project, and they deserve our public thanks: Chris Kepner, Dawn Goldsmith and each of our children: Joe and Briana (and the little guys), Brendon, Ari and Zach; and Sophie and Elena.

To all of you: thank you and cheers!

CHRONOLOGY OF EVENTS

ca. 900   A group of indigenous people settle in the area now known as Philippe Park. They are later referred to as the Tocobaga.

1528   Pánfilo de Narváez lands near Tampa Bay and likely visits the Tocobaga village in what is now Safety Harbor on his way north through the Florida interior. Narváez and all but four of his men perish during the expedition.

1539   Hernando de Soto sets off to explore the New World and disembarks on the west coast of Florida, believed to be at or near Tampa Bay.

1549   Fray (Father) Luis Cancer de Barbastro travels to the west coast of Florida, more than likely Tampa Bay, to perform missionary work. He is killed by the Tocobaga shortly after his arrival.

1567   Pedro Menéndez de Avilés negotiates a peace treaty between the Calusa and the Tocobaga peoples, at a village believed to be located in present-day Safety Harbor. Before leaving, Menéndez establishes a fort near the Tocobaga village. A year later, the fort is found destroyed.

1821   Florida is purchased from Spain and becomes a U.S. territory.

1842   The U.S. Congress passes the Armed Occupation Act, offering 160 acres in parts of Florida free of charge under certain conditions. The Act soon leads to the settlement of the Pinellas peninsula. Pursuant to the Act, Odet Philippe becomes the first person of European descent to lawfully settle on the Pinellas peninsula, establishing a plantation called St. Helena in what is now known as Philippe Park.

1848   A devastating hurricane pummels Tampa Bay, widely considered the worst to hit the region. Odet Philippe's home and groves are destroyed.

1853   Odet W. "Keeter" Booth, Philippe's grandson and the son of settler Richard Booth, becomes the first person of European descent born on the Pinellas peninsula.

ca. 1853   James P. "Captain Jim" McMullen establishes the first school on the Pinellas peninsula, a few miles west of the growing settlement. The school is named for the teacher's child, a girl named Sylvan Abbey.

1855   The Espiritu Santo Springs are purchased from the U.S. government by Colonel William J. Bailey Jr.

1869   Odet Philippe dies.

ca. 1890   The community becomes known as Green Springs. The settlement's first post office is established, with Sid Youngblood serving as the first postmaster.

1895   Early pioneer and Civil War veteran James P. "Captain Jim" McMullen passes away.

ca. 1900   Bailey's son-in-law James F. Tucker, a former captain of the Confederacy during the Civil War, begins making improvements to the springs by erecting a pavilion around the swimming tank and installing pumps to better attract vacationers and those seeking treatment through use of the restorative waters.

ca. 1905   The Tocobaga mound located near the Lover's Oak tree is destroyed and the shells within it removed for use on county roads.

1912   Pinellas County secedes from Hillsborough County.

1914   The first railroad connecting Safety Harbor, Clearwater and St. Petersburg is completed.

1915   The town's first newspaper, the *Tropical Breeze*, makes its debut. After one year, it is discontinued and replaced by the *Safety Harbor Herald*, published by A.E. Shower.

1916   A schoolhouse is built in Safety Harbor for students from first through ninth grades.

1917   The city is incorporated as the City of Safety Harbor. Less than three months later, on September 1, many buildings are destroyed when a fire consumes Main Street.

1921   A major hurricane strikes the region. The pavilion and dance hall on the pier are destroyed, as well as several structures previously constructed at the springs.

1925   The St. James Hotel opens.

1926   An alleged smallpox epidemic threatens the city's black community.

1927   Safety Harbor organizes its first volunteer fire department.

1928   Dr. Con F. Barth opens Dr. Barth's Hotel & Baths, a hotel and health establishment north of the Espiritu Santo Springs.

1930   Dr. Matthew W. Stirling, an ethnologist at the Smithsonian Institution, excavates the Tocobaga site in Philippe Park. He finds pottery, Spanish artifacts dating from the sixteenth century and a significant number of human remains.

1935   Another storm destroys the Safety Harbor pier and the old railroad bridge to Oldsmar. The same year, the Davis Causeway is completed across Tampa Bay, diverting traffic away from the city.

1936   Dr. Alben Jansik, an Austrian physician, purchases the facility at Espiritu Santo Springs at a tax sale. At first the resort thrives under Dr. Jansik's control, but within a few years, it is used primarily as a rehabilitation facility for wealthy recovering alcoholics.

1937   The City of Safety Harbor declares bankruptcy. Still, the city will be handcuffed by its outstanding debt for the next several decades.

1938   With funding received from the Works Progress Administration, the city's first public library is established, with Mrs. Daisy Cahow serving as librarian.

1945	Dr. Salem Baranoff purchases the facilities at Espiritu Santo Springs and renames the property the Safety Harbor Spa.
1948	Following the death of landowner Thomas Palmer, Philippe Park is established by Pinellas County. Further excavations are then performed at the Tocobaga village site by Ripley Bullen and John Griffin, two archaeologists of the Florida Park Service. Bullen and Griffin unearth pottery and stone tools produced by the Tocobaga, as well as several more European artifacts.
1957	Mayor Ben Downs declares a citywide emergency and fires the city's chief of police and building inspector. The following day, a court rules that Downs lacked the authority to take this action and orders the men reinstated. By the end of the year, an election to recall Downs will be held. He will survive.
1959	Three armed men rob a safe containing $200,000 in cash, checks and jewelry at the Safety Harbor Spa.
1963	Passenger service is ended at the Safety Harbor railroad depot after business at the station declines.
1964	William Blackshear is elected as a city commissioner, becoming the first African American to hold public office in Safety Harbor and possibly statewide since the end of Reconstruction. That same year, the Safety Harbor Spa is designated a historical landmark by the U.S. Department of the Interior.
1976	The Safety Harbor Police Department is abolished.
1985	Hurricane Elena causes extensive damage to Safety Harbor totaling nearly $4 million.
1986	A car is driven onto the newly renovated pier and set aflame.
1994	A new public library is built on Second Street North. Later, the building's space is expanded by 60 percent.
2004	The Olympia Development Group purchases the Safety Harbor Resort and Spa for $25 million.
2013	The city's new waterfront park, located north of the pier, opens to the public. Also this year, construction of the Safety Harbor Art and Music Center is expected to be completed.

INTRODUCTION

At just five square miles, the city of Safety Harbor might seem to be a curious choice for the subject of a full-length history book. Yet despite its limited size, Safety Harbor can boast a robust, vibrant past. For more than five hundred years, due to easy access to the waters of Tampa Bay and its plentiful sea life, the Tocobaga people lived along its shores, from where they eventually became the dominant power of the region. In the sixteenth century, Spanish explorers and missionaries arrived in the area, seeking riches and a safe haven for the transport of goods from Mexico and to introduce the indigenous population to Christianity.

Later, in the mid-nineteenth century, Safety Harbor's strategic location and fertile farmland attracted pioneers seeking a new life. One of those early settlers, Odet Philippe, was greatly responsible for the development of Florida's citrus industry, planting groves of oranges and lemons on the land that once housed the Tocobaga village, while sharing his knowledge with his new neighbors. The natural mineral springs drew visitors to bathe in their restorative waters, and at the turn of the twentieth century, a pavilion and swimming tank were constructed that were eventually transformed into the world-famous Safety Harbor Resort and Spa, enjoyed by wealthy industrialists, socialites, and professional athletes for decades.

Pinellas County hangs down off the middle of Florida's west coast like a crooked thumb, serving as the natural barrier between Tampa Bay on the east and the Gulf of Mexico on the west. Known for its year-round temperate weather, white sand beaches and abundant bird life, Pinellas

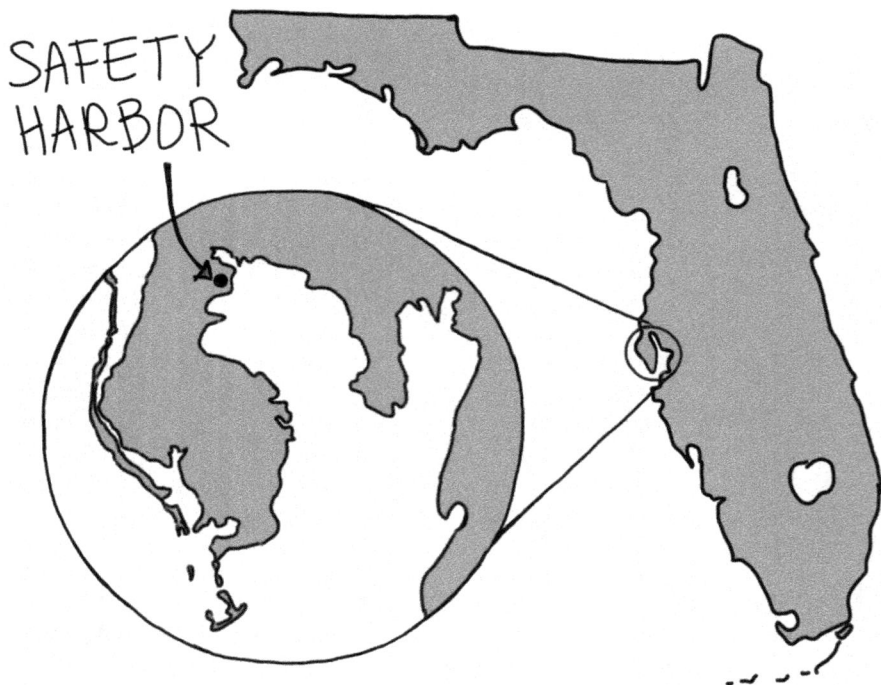

Map depicting the location of Safety Harbor in relation to the state of Florida and Pinellas County. *Drawing by Ari Kepner.*

County is also the most densely populated county in Florida, surpassing even Miami's Dade County.

The city of Safety Harbor is situated along the eastern edge of this peninsula, on the western bank of Old Tampa Bay, advantageously positioned between the major commercial centers of the region. Twenty miles east, across the Courtney Campbell Causeway, is Tampa, nicknamed the "Cigar City," and the same distance south lies St. Petersburg, the "Sunshine City." Ten miles west is downtown Clearwater and its famous beaches, while Tarpon Springs, the "Sponge City," sits approximately fifteen miles to the north.

Safety Harbor is not without its own sobriquet, either, once widely known as the "Health Giving City, where the healing waters flow." The city has long been defined by its natural mineral springs, which some believe were first discovered by Hernando de Soto and thought by him to be the elusive and mythical Fountain of Youth.

During the first half of the twentieth century, the city straddled the dissimilar worlds of pioneer Florida and the new era that was marked by development and technological advancement, as reflected in an article appearing in the *Safety Harbor Herald* on February 5, 1926:

> *Picture if you can this city yesterday—it was but yesterday that Safety Harbor was a sleepy cross-roads village, slumbering in the everlasting sunshine at the intersection of two winding sand roads. A few wooden buildings sufficed to house the scant population and the few stores necessary to serve their needs. The streets were mere paths, often overgrown with weeds and rank tropical growth. In attractions for the stranger there were none and the whisperings of the waters of Old Tampa Bay on the white sands of the beach carried its alluring message only to the ears of the few idlers forever basking in the sun around the village shores. This was but yesterday—a few short years ago and today a miracle of progress greets the eye. Tall, modern apartments, pavilion, sanitarium, hotels and bright shiny shops now mark the intersection of the sand roads, now changed as if by the wand of a fairy to wide smooth boulevards. This is a glimpse of today. Tomorrow—the day of mystery to him who cannot see—cannot envision in his mind the changes which the future may bring to pass. But to him of the open mind and imagination of things to come, tomorrow holds no*

Estimated to be between three hundred and five hundred years old, the Baranoff Oak is believed to be the oldest live oak tree in Pinellas County and serves as a visible landmark near the Safety Harbor Public Library. *Photo by Terrie Thomas.*

From the Safety Harbor Pier, visitors can enjoy views of Old Tampa Bay and possibly catch a glimpse of manatees, stingrays and dolphins. *Photo by Terrie Thomas.*

> *mysteries. For here is a city in the making, as yet young, scarcely out of the swaddling clothes of infancy, yet with the tangible evidence before the eyes that today the future holds as much as did the future of yesterday. The day of opportunity in Safety Harbor has just begun.*

That "day of opportunity" described by *Herald* editor A.E. Shower did come, bringing with it modern subdivisions and the creation of a library, a historical museum and an extensive system of parks and recreation facilities. Today, the city is known for its abundance of festivals and the collection of artists, musicians, writers and poets who call it their home—an oasis of calm within bustling Pinellas County.

More than anything else, though, Safety Harbor is marked by the ubiquitous spirit of community that has existed since the settlement's beginnings. In 1966, Gladys Ganley, a longtime resident and descendant of the regional pioneers, wrote of those early days: "A spirit of good will and fellowship pervaded the entire community. Anyone suffering a sickness or a disaster was cheerfully helped by all the neighbors. A feeling of comradeship among the early settlers, exists among their descendants to this day." Nearly fifty years later, it still does.

In the pages that follow, we hope to provide a glimpse into the history and energy that infuse this special city on the edge of Tampa Bay. We have attempted to present the fullest account possible and to depict life as it existed during each stage of the city's rich past, but there is undoubtedly much more to tell. We invite you to visit our web site, www.historyofsafetyharbor.com, to record your personal memories and stories of your experiences in Safety Harbor for others to enjoy.

PART I
BEFORE THE FIRST SETTLERS

WAS HE OR WASN'T HE?

The Enduring Myth of Hernando de Soto and the Espiritu Santo Springs

On May 18, 1539, Spanish explorer Hernando De Soto reached the shores of what is now Tampa Bay, landing near these mineral springs used by the native population for nearly 10,000 years. Believing he had found the legendary Fountain of Youth somehow missed by Ponce de León, De Soto established a camp here, naming the crystal clear waters Espiritu Santo Springs—"Springs of the Holy Spirit."
—excerpt from a historical marker in front of the Safety Harbor Resort and Spa

According to local lore, in May 1539, approximately one week after setting sail from Cuba, famed Spanish explorer Hernando de Soto entered Tampa Bay at the start of his historic expedition to explore the land then known simply as La Florida. In honor of the holy day of Pentecost Sunday, he named the body of water *Bahia Espiritu Santo*—the "Bay of the Holy Spirit." There, in what is now Safety Harbor, de Soto and his men discovered five mineral springs gushing from the sand, springs that were believed by the indigenous inhabitants of the nearby village of Ucita to hold special healing properties and were perhaps even the mythical Fountain of Youth that was so eagerly (and unsuccessfully) sought by de Soto's countryman Ponce de León.

It was a startling beginning to de Soto's journey, hinting at the riches that he would surely find during the coming months and years. Yet de Soto could hardly have suspected what was ahead: that his expedition would roam aimlessly through what is now the southeastern United States, eventually

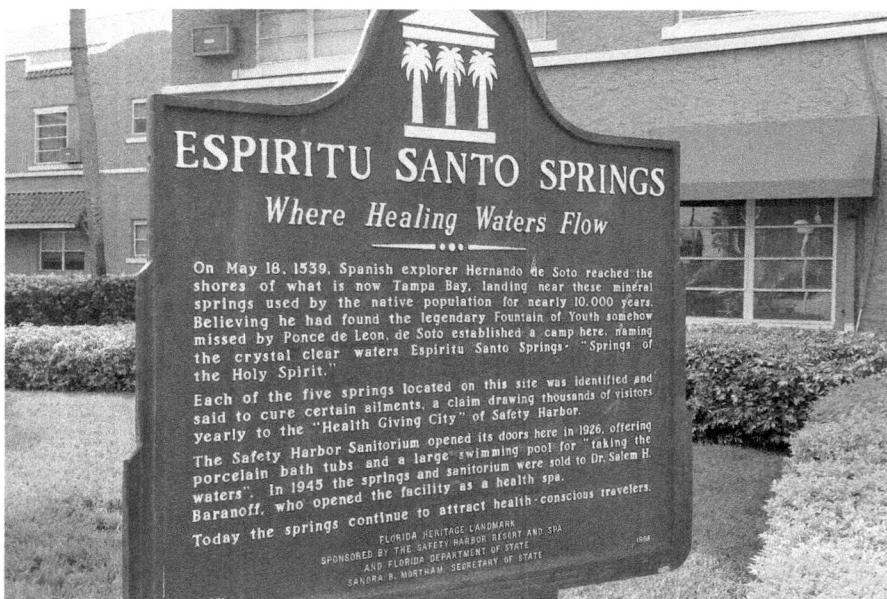

A historical marker in front of the Safety Harbor Resort and Spa describes the alleged visit by Hernando de Soto in 1539. *Photo by Warren Firschein.*

climaxing with the discovery of the Rio Grande de la Florida—the Mississippi River—along whose banks de Soto would die almost exactly three years later without finding the wealth that had lured him there.

Despite the ultimate failure of de Soto's expedition, Safety Harbor's historical legacy had been firmly established as the location of de Soto's initial landing point and the site of the first indigenous settlement encountered by his party. The legend of de Soto's arrival and discovery of the city's natural springs, identified by him as the Fountain of Youth, endures to this day. The city has long seized upon and promoted this past. During the 1930s, for example, a physical depiction of de Soto dramatically pointed the way to Safety Harbor from atop a nearby road sign. Today, a historical marker erected on the grounds of the Safety Harbor Resort and Spa describes his visit to the area.

But just how much of this story is true? As it turns out, not much.

THE EXPEDITION OF HERNANDO DE SOTO

This is what is known:

In 1537, after returning home from an expedition to conquer Peru, Hernando de Soto was commissioned by King Charles V of Spain to explore the land known as La Florida. De Soto's primary mission was to conquer, pacify and settle a large section of Florida's coast and establish a colony to serve as a supply port for Spanish ships operating in the Gulf of Mexico and the Caribbean. De Soto's charter specifically required that he bring with him five hundred men and that he construct three stone forts using his own funds in the process. Based on the fabulous wealth found in

Portrait of Hernando de Soto (circa 1497–1542) from 1791. *Courtesy of Library of Congress.*

Central and South America by other Spanish expeditions, he was also intent on searching for gold and precious jewels, for he was entitled to retain a share of the colony's profits in addition to receiving titles and lands for his efforts. An ancillary goal was to help Spain establish a protected overland route between the Gulf and the Atlantic coast to transport goods from Mexico. At that time, the only method for shipping cargo from Mexico was by sea, which had proven dangerous. Already a number of Spanish ships had been lost in the waters off Florida, and it was believed that such a route from Mexico would be safer.

De Soto was not the first Spanish explorer to pass through the region; approximately ten years earlier, Pánfilo de Narváez had landed near Tampa Bay, reputedly at present-day St. Petersburg, and led a party of roughly three hundred men north through the interior of Florida. That earlier expedition was a disaster, however, ultimately claiming the lives of Narváez and all but four of his men. About a year later, a rescue party searching for Narváez sailed into the bay. Several soldiers from this rescue party were captured by members of the local indigenous population, and as it turned out, one survived.

Such was the backdrop when, on or around May 18, 1539, de Soto set sail for Florida from Havana, Cuba. Determined not to make the same mistakes as Narváez, de Soto had sought the counsel of Alvar Núñez Cabeza de Vaca, one of the few survivors of that catastrophic expedition. From Cabeza de Vaca, de Soto had learned of some of the challenges to be faced in the Florida interior. Based on this insight, he brought along with him several times the number of Narváez's group, estimated between six hundred and one thousand people in total.

De Soto's expedition was almost a city in itself. It included more than just soldiers: there were nobility and relatives of de Soto, tradesmen and merchants, as well as apprentices, pages, servants and slaves. Women were used as servants, and Africans served as bodyguards for the Spanish nobility. Priests and friars were included, too, both for the spiritual well-being of the expedition and to convert the indigenous people to Christianity. In addition, they had with them various types of animals, including horses, mules and war dogs. Because Cabeza de Vaca had reported how the Narváez expedition had struggled to find food, de Soto also brought pigs—some of which would later escape to form the wild hog population that still plagues parts of the southeastern United States. It took five large vessels and four smaller ones to transport them all.

The expedition sailed north for approximately a week—the exact number of days remains in doubt—before finding a suitable place to disembark. Upon landing, de Soto soon reached an American Indian village called Ucita, where he established a small fortified compound that served as his first North American headquarters. Nearby, he discovered a Spaniard named Juan Ortiz, who explained that he was a member of the party that had set out to rescue Narváez years earlier. Ortiz told de Soto that he had been enslaved in the area ever since his capture. De Soto stayed at his compound near Ucita for about six weeks before he moved north, leaving behind a few soldiers at the garrison.

Controversy Over de Soto's Landing Point

Over the years, historians and archaeologists have conducted an astonishing amount of scholarly research in an effort to identify de Soto's initial landing point and the location of the village of Ucita. In Safety Harbor, local legend insists that Ucita was the name given to the Tocobaga settlement whose ruins can be found today in the city's Philippe Park. At one time, this claim had widespread support. For example, in a seminal 1929 text on the history of Pinellas County, William Straub, former editor of the *St. Petersburg Times*, described Safety Harbor as "the recognized landing place of De Soto, who with his brave crew and embued [*sic*] with the spirit of chivalry, the spirit of discovery and the hopes of all Spain, sailed into the beautiful land-locked bay one bright Sunday morning back in May, 1539." In a 1938 article published in the *Florida Historical Quarterly*, Mark F. Boyd persuasively argued that the Tocobaga village in Philippe Park best fit descriptions of Ucita and the topography of the immediate region that had been made by members of the de Soto expedition.

But no tangible evidence supports this claim. Because of the large number of people on the expedition and the length of their stay at their compound, logic suggests that some physical record of their presence should still exist, even after nearly half a millennium. Although a limited number of Spanish artifacts have been discovered during archaeological excavations in Philippe Park, based on what has been unearthed, it is simply not credible that up to one thousand Europeans camped there for approximately six weeks' time. This, by itself, does not eliminate Safety Harbor as de Soto's possible landing point, for no archaeological evidence has been uncovered *anywhere* that would unambiguously identify the location of de Soto's initial headquarters and the village of Ucita.

With the absence of physical evidence, historians have studied surviving documents for clues. Four different participants in the de Soto expedition later produced written accounts of the journey that are known today. In addition, de Soto himself penned a long letter from his first encampment that describes the village of Ucita. Unfortunately, these sources provide limited detail and often conflict with one another on basic information such as distance, time and direction, making it truly impossible to determine the expedition's exact route and location at any given time.

Using what little can be gleaned from those reports, such as descriptions of the landscape and geography of the surrounding area, researchers over the years have suggested a number of different locations along the southwestern coast of Florida that they consider the most likely possible sites of the first encampment and the village of Ucita. These include Terra Ceia Island on the southeast side of Tampa Bay in Manatee County; Charlotte Harbor, near modern-day Fort Myers; and the mouth of the Little Manatee River, near Ruskin. Each has its supporters and detractors.

Possibly buttressing Safety Harbor's claim are descriptions of the village and nearby landscape made by participants of the de Soto expedition that appear to match the local area, factors cited by Mark Boyd in his 1938 article mentioned earlier. Then there is also the strange case of Juan Ortiz, the Spaniard from the Narváez rescue party. It is widely believed that after Narváez landed at Tampa Bay, he and his party passed through a large village with a high mound located on the shore of the bay, which some historians believe was the Tocobaga settlement in Philippe Park. There, the indigenous peoples showed him corn and items salvaged from a Spanish ship, including gold. Later, the rescue party in search of Narváez located a village that they believed he had previously visited, and it was here where Ortiz was captured and held by the chief of Ucita. After being rescued himself, Ortiz reportedly told de Soto that he had never traveled more than ten leagues from the site of his original captivity years earlier. But these points do not necessarily suggest that the village of Ucita was located in Safety Harbor, or even that de Soto landed in Pinellas County. For one thing, even if Narváez visited the village in Philippe Park, this was not necessarily the place where Ortiz was captured. Ucita was described as a fairly small village, while Safety Harbor is the site of one of the largest, if not *the* largest, known American Indian settlement in the Greater Tampa Bay region. Even if Ortiz was captured near Philippe Park, however, he may have been relocated or journeyed to the east side of Tampa Bay before he was found. Ortiz reported that when he learned that he was to be killed by the Ucitans, he escaped into the territory of another chief named Mocoso, which is presumably where he was ultimately discovered.

Experts continue to passionately contest the route of de Soto's expedition. In 1993, using more recent research tools and archaeological information than was previously available to historians, renowned authorities Jerald Milanich and Charles Hudson constructed a convincing case that de Soto's landing point (and the site of Ucita) was near the mouth of the Little Manatee River, on the east side of Tampa Bay, roughly parallel to the southern tip of the Pinellas peninsula. Unfortunately, the site has been long since destroyed, likely to obtain shell material used to pave roads, thereby making it impossible to prove this hypothesis. Yet descriptions of the area made prior to its destruction match those by the de Soto chroniclers, and it "is the only location that satisfies all the locational requirements" described in the historical literature. Milanich and Hudson themselves admit, however, that "[a]bsolute archaeological proof that the de Soto expedition camp was located on the north side of the Little Manatee River…is not available."

The bottom line is that without definitive physical evidence, each place named here has as much claim to being de Soto's landing point as the others. Historians can agree only that de Soto and his army landed somewhere along the southwestern coast of Florida and that the precise location of his first encampment (and that of the village of Ucita) "remains in doubt."

Although the truth may never be known, the story that de Soto reached Safety Harbor and discovered its mineral springs persists and has been a vibrant part of the city's lore since the early days of the community. A local pamphlet printed in 1910 proclaimed that the Espiritu Santo Springs are "the Original 'Fountain of Perpetual Youth' Sought for by Ponce de León, and Discovered by Hernando De Soto in May, 1539." This belief was so widely held that in December 1936, and prior to the publication of the U.S. government's Final Report of the United States De Soto Expedition Commission, a group of prominent local residents traveled to Tampa in an effort to convince a member of that commission that de Soto disembarked at Safety Harbor, specifically citing the presence of the Tocobaga village, the mineral springs and a landlocked harbor, among other things mentioned by the original de Soto chroniclers. That a contrary conclusion was ultimately reached by the De Soto Commission did nothing to quell enthusiasm for the idea. In 1947, for example, an article in the *Tampa Tribune* by columnist D.B. McKay insisted that de Soto landed on the west side of Tampa Bay, near downtown Safety Harbor. Curiously enough, there is no evidence to suggest that either Ponce de León or Hernando de Soto were even searching for the Fountain of Youth in the first place. That story was most likely invented years after de León's expedition by a Spanish historian named Gonzalo Fernández de Oviedo in 1535, allegedly in an attempt to make de León appear foolish.[1] Whatever its origins, however, this tale has become a part of the city's back-story.

---

1. According to Dr. Michael Francis, while Oviedo praised explorers like Christopher Columbus and Hernando Cortés, he denigrated others, including Juan Ponce de León, for their greed, superstition and stupidity: "According to Oviedo, Ponce was a vain man, prone to pursue silly ventures that enhanced his own ego, no matter the cost. To illustrate this point, Oviedo claimed that a group of Indians in the Caribbean had deceived Ponce and his followers, leading them to believe that an enchanted spring was hidden somewhere in the islands of Bimini (the Bahamas), and that its waters made men young again. Convinced the rumors were true, Ponce and his men wandered aimlessly among the islands for six months, Oviedo claimed. Continuing to mock Ponce's gullibility, Oviedo claimed that he himself had witnessed first-hand how old men could turn young, something that was achieved without the assistance of any fountain; rather, the transformation was caused simply by a weakening of the brain, which made grown men behave like young boys who possessed little reason or understanding. This, Oviedo claimed, was precisely what had happened to Ponce de León." Eventually, concludes Dr. Francis, "what began as myth has slowly transformed into historical fact." Many history texts continue to report this story as true.

Chapter 2

THE TRAGIC END OF
FRAY LUIS CANCER DE BARBASTRO

A bove the doors to the sanctuary at Safety Harbor's Espiritu Santo Catholic Church hangs a stained-glass window depicting a sixteenth-century Spanish Catholic priest. In the image, the priest can be seen standing in a body of water holding a cross high with one hand, while being discreetly watched from afar by a group of indigenous people. Not far away, at the main entrance of the church, a Catholic Heritage Marker provides the identity of this man: he is a famed Dominican missionary named Father Luis Cancer, who was martyred nearby "in an attempt to spread the Gospel among the native peoples."

Cancer's story is a fascinating and cautionary tale that reveals some of the challenges faced by Spanish explorers and missionaries during the mid-sixteenth century. Unlike the Narváez and de Soto excursions, however, the purpose of this

A stained-glass window at Safety Harbor's Espiritu Santo Catholic Church depicts the martyrdom of Fray Luis Cancer de Barbastro. *Photo by Dawn Goldsmith.*

trip was not to seek riches or construct new Spanish settlements but solely to introduce the indigenous population to Christianity.

THE MISSION OF FRAY LUIS CANCER

After de Soto, the next official Spanish expedition to visit the west coast of the Florida peninsula was led by the devoted missionary Fray (Father) Luis Cancer de Barbastro, sometimes written as Luis de Cancer. Unlike earlier Spanish explorers, Fray Cancer believed that the indigenous people should be treated with dignity and respect instead of being subjected to fear and intimidation. This mindset had already proven to be profoundly successful during Cancer's prior missions to convert native people to Christianity. In what is now Guatemala, for example, his efforts were so well received that before long "the whole region had exchanged idols and weaponry for the cross," as described by essayist Gene Burnett.

Although the indigenous peoples had already been treated savagely by the Narváez and de Soto expeditions and were generally regarded as hostile, Fray Cancer believed that additional violence would be futile in attempting to convert American Indians to Christianity and that his techniques would work in La Florida as well. In 1547, King Charles V approved Cancer's proposal to conduct a peaceful mission to Florida.

Yet despite his focus on converting the local population through "gentleness instead of force," Cancer was not naïve. He understood that his mission would have the greatest chance of success by working with those indigenous Floridians who had not been previously subjected to such poor treatment. Cancer therefore had the viceroy of Mexico instruct his pilot, Juan de Arana, to avoid the regions where Spaniards had previously made contact with indigenous people. Unfortunately, Cancer would soon learn that he was right to be cautious, and his care would be for naught.

THE UNFORTUNATE FATE OF FRAY CANCER'S EXPEDITION

Two years later, in the spring of 1549, Fray Cancer and a small party that included three other Dominican friars left Veracruz, Mexico. They stopped in Havana, where they stocked up on food and supplies and were provided with a potentially more valuable asset: an American Indian slave woman from Florida named Magdalena who had since converted to Christianity and would serve as their translator.

The expedition then left on its mission. But either intentionally or mistakenly, their pilot ignored the instructions to avoid Florida's Gulf Coast and brought them to approximately the same place where Narváez and de Soto had landed years earlier.

At first, Cancer's apprehension appeared to be unwarranted. Upon making their first landing, the expedition encountered a group of apparently peaceful people who told the missionaries about their villages, which were located near a harbor approximately a day and a half away. These Floridians are believed to have been the Tocobaga, a group of indigenous people who lived in small villages scattered throughout the Tampa Bay region, including in what is now Safety Harbor's Philippe Park.

This open welcome did not last long. As Fray Cancer returned to the ship to obtain more presents for the Tocobaga, Magdalena and two of the friars vanished from the shore. One of the expedition's sailors, who was with them, disappeared as well. Cancer and the remaining friar searched the shoreline in vain, unable to locate any sign of the missing Spaniards or the Tocobaga. They were alone. With limited options, Cancer and the friar returned to the ship and sailed north with the crew in search of the villages they had been told about.

The ship reached a wide bay on June 23, 1549. There, along the shore, Cancer and his remaining contingent discovered Magdalena and a group of Tocobaga. But Magdalena had evidently changed. She was no longer wearing her Spanish-issued clothing and was now dressed in native attire—a "brief native moss skirt," according to one source. Unashamed by her transformation, she informed Cancer that the missing friars and sailor were relaxing safely at the nearby village, where they were enjoying the hospitality of the local chief. Moreover, she reported that she had convinced the Tocobaga that Cancer and the friars had come on a peaceful mission and that as many as fifty or sixty of their number had gathered to hear what the missionaries had to tell them.

Overjoyed by this turn of events, Fray Cancer returned to the ship to prepare for this meeting. But back on board, he was greeted by a surprise: a Spanish sailor named Juan Muñoz, who had been living among the Tocobaga for the past ten years. Muñoz, it turned out, was one of the soldiers who had stayed behind at the garrison constructed by the Hernando de Soto expedition while the majority of the expedition continued northward.

Muñoz explained that he had been captured by the Tocobaga and had been held as a slave ever since. If true, this story would seem to support the contention that Cancer had accidentally arrived close to de Soto's landing point, wherever that may have been. But Muñoz had not come to reminisce. Noticing Cancer's ship floating in the bay, Muñoz had used the opportunity to escape from his master by paddling out in a canoe.

Muñoz quickly reported the bad news: the two friars who had been with Magdalena had been killed, and the sailor who had accompanied them had been enslaved. Magdalena had lied to them.

Upon hearing this, the sailors and missionaries remaining on the ship tried to persuade Cancer to return to Mexico immediately. Cancer, however, was unmoved. He reminded them of their commitment to the missionary project, thereby unwittingly sealing his own fate.

The next day, accompanied by Muñoz and the remaining friar, Fray Cancer rowed toward shore. As they neared land, they noticed a group of hostile Tocobaga brandishing weapons and demanding the release of their slave, Juan Muñoz. Despite the obvious danger, Cancer jumped overboard and swam ashore, ignoring the friar's pleas to return to the safety of the boat.

Upon reaching land, Cancer approached the group of Tocobaga, who were gathered together on a small hill. This hill was perhaps a man-made earthen mound, a common feature of local indigenous villages. As he arrived, several of them rushed forward and pushed him down the incline. Then, while Muñoz and the friar watched in horror, one of the Tocobaga violently pulled off the hat Cancer was wearing and another proceeded to beat him to death with a wooden club. The remainder of Cancer's party left Tampa Bay two days later and returned to Mexico.

"Cancer's death," wrote Michael J. McNally, "put an end to Spanish attempts to evangelize without the presence of soldiers."

SPECULATION ABOUT WHY FRAY CANCER WAS KILLED

The reason behind the Tocobaga's violent behavior toward Fray Cancer and his men remains a mystery, for the Tocobaga held a reputation as a generally peaceful people. The most widely accepted theory is that their hostile actions were a reaction to the treatment previously experienced at the hands of the Spanish. The Narváez and de Soto expeditions were notoriously cruel to the indigenous populations. In addition, Cuban fishermen and vessels engaged in illegal slaving had likely made periodic informal contact with the indigenous peoples throughout the first half of the sixteenth century. There is some documentary evidence indicating that indigenous peoples were sporadically transported to Cuba during the early and middle parts of the sixteenth century, particularly from the west-central coast of the Florida peninsula. Quite possibly, Magdalena was enslaved in this manner. This theory, however, wouldn't appear to explain why the Tocobaga were initially peaceful when first encountered by Cancer and his party.

A second possible explanation focuses on the former member of the de Soto expedition, Juan Muñoz. If the Tocobaga were, in fact, "shouting for the release of their slave" when the Spaniards approached the shore in their small boat, it wouldn't be unreasonable to deduce that they decided to retaliate against Cancer for aiding Muñoz's escape. But this explanation fails to explain why the Tocobaga reportedly attacked and killed the other two friars *before* Muñoz paddled off in his canoe.

There is a third potential explanation, however, and for this, we have to consider the possible motivation of the Indian interpreter, the woman called Magdalena. This was a woman who had previously been spirited away from her homeland and enslaved among the Spaniards in Cuba. Now, at long last, she had an opportunity to return to her people. Historians will never know what Magdalena told the Tocobaga, but we can imagine her describing the cruelty the Spaniards had exhibited toward her and the local population and pleading with them to help her escape and return home. Perhaps she somehow manipulated the Tocobaga into engaging in aggressive behavior and performing murder. This is all merely speculation, but we know that Magdalena didn't hesitate to reassert her old identity by changing her attire at the first opportunity. We also know that she lied to Fray Cancer, maintaining that the rest of her party was safe when, in fact, they had already been killed or enslaved. No one will ever know the truth, but it is worth noting that Magdalena evidently disappeared and did not return to Cuba with the remaining men.

Today, Fray Luis Cancer de Barbastro is considered the "Proto-Martyr of Florida"—the first missionary to give his life in bringing Christianity to the indigenous peoples of Florida. Although the precise location of Cancer's death is not known, there are few hills or earthen mounds that are visible from the waters of Tampa Bay, and one of these is the large mound located in present-day Philippe Park. As a result, it is not implausible to believe that this site may have been the location of the events described here.

Chapter 3

PEDRO MENÉNDEZ DE AVILÉS AND THE CALUSA-TOCOBAGA PEACE TREATY

S eventeen years passed before Tampa Bay received another European visitor. Before his arrival, Spanish explorer and missionary Pedro Menéndez de Avilés had founded the city of St. Augustine, recognized as the first permanent European settlement in the United States, during a successful mission to oust the French from La Florida before they could establish their own colony. On this voyage, however, he had a different sort of mission in mind. Menéndez planned to visit the Calusa, a powerful, prosperous indigenous people who lived along the coastal areas of southwest Florida, roughly from Charlotte Harbor down to the southernmost part of the Florida peninsula. The primary goal of Menéndez's voyage was to search for a water passage linking the east and west coasts of the peninsula. At the same time, he would attempt to secure the release of Spanish shipwreck survivors living among the Calusa, one of whom Menéndez believed might have been his own son. In addition, he would try to convert some of the Calusa to Catholicism, which was often an ancillary goal for many of the Spanish explorers during this period.

The Calusa were not unknown to the Spanish in 1566. The culture had been first encountered by Spanish explorers over fifty years earlier, in 1513, when Ponce de León anchored near Charlotte Harbor and was immediately attacked by eighty canoes of Calusa warriors. From that time forward, the Calusa were recognized as the largest and most powerful group of indigenous people in South Florida. Their principal town of Calus (located near Fort Myers Beach today) is believed to have had a population of about one thousand individuals, while between four and seven thousand other Calusa

Portrait of Pedro
Menéndez de Avilés
(1519–1574) by
Francisco de Paula
Martí (1761–1827).
*Courtesy of Library of
Congress.*

probably lived in approximately fifty smaller villages scattered along the coast. Later, when de León returned to the southwest coast in 1521 with two ships containing two hundred men, his party was attacked by the Calusa, and de León himself was mortally wounded. So Menéndez undoubtedly had a good sense of the challenges that awaited him.

The chief of the Calusa was a man named Calus, or possible Calos or Caalus, which meant "fierce" or "brave" in their language. The Spanish corrupted this name into something more understandable to them and simply called him Carlos.

Once Menéndez arrived, Carlos allowed the Spanish to establish a small outpost and a Jesuit mission near his capital of Calus village and reluctantly released his captive shipwreck survivors. Yet Carlos schemed to use the Spanish might for his own political advantage. After pressuring Menéndez to marry his sister, Carlos deceptively told Menéndez that he knew of a water passage connecting the Florida coasts. It was located in the territory of the Tocobaga, the tribe that controlled the area north of Calusa territory around Tampa Bay and the one that is believed to have been tragically encountered by Fray Cancer seventeen years earlier. Not incidentally, the Tocobaga also happened to be the Calusa's major rival for power along the west coast during this period and their sworn enemies as well. All Menéndez had to do to gain access to this waterway was to help Carlos destroy the Tocobaga, thereby allowing the Calusa to extend their territory north into the central west coast.

To his credit, Menéndez refused to accommodate Carlos's ambition. Instead of acquiescing to Carlos's suggestion, he told the Calusa chief that he would negotiate a peace treaty between the two tribes. Although frustrated by Menéndez's apparent lack of enthusiasm for battle, Carlos reluctantly agreed to comply with the Spaniard's proposal and consented to accompany Menéndez to the Tocobaga territory with some of his men to make peace.[2]

---

2. This approach of seeking a peace treaty might seem to conflict with the commonly held views of Menéndez, who suffers from a poor reputation regarding his treatment of the indigenous people throughout Florida. In fact, a few years later, in 1572, he would urge the Spanish crown to engage in a "war of extermination" against the Florida Indians. But at this time, his behavior toward the native population was quite different. Indeed, as explained by anthropologist John Goggin, "Menéndez himself tried to treat the Indians fairly, making special efforts to settle disputes between them and giving no aggressive cause for displeasure on his part" and instructed his soldiers not to attack or plunder their villages. Despite his best intentions, however, he could not prevent his men from assaulting the American Indians and destroying their property or well-intentioned missionaries from offending their beliefs and customs. The indigenous peoples soon retaliated, driving Spanish forces from some areas entirely. Eventually, "[u]nable to understand the natives' motives, Menéndez and his compatriots decided that the coastal tribes of Florida were naturally treacherous and deceitful—'warlike' and of 'bad disposition,' as one Spaniard put it," and urged Spain to undertake "a war of fire and blood" against them. *See* David J. Weber, *The Spanish Frontier in North America* (New Haven, CT: Yale University Press, 1992), page 74. But that would happen in 1572—well after (and partially as a result of) his experience with the Calusa.

Menéndez Meets with the Tocobaga

With Carlos and twenty of his warriors on board, Menéndez sailed for the Tocobaga territory and their principal village. He also brought with him several translators, including a Spaniard who was being held captive by Carlos and knew both the Calusa and Tocobaga languages. They reached the edge of the village without being noticed. Recognizing his opportunity, Carlos pleaded with Menéndez to let them land, burn the village, and kill the Tocobaga. Once again, Menéndez refused these appeals, explaining that, as Christians, they were required to attempt to make peace between the tribes. Menéndez then promised Carlos that he would negotiate for the release of Calusa prisoners held by the Tocobaga. This offer appeared to satisfy the Calusa chief, at least for the moment.

The following day, Menéndez and Carlos entered the village with Spanish soldiers, Calusa warriors and the translators to meet with the Tocobaga. Word of their arrival spread throughout the territory. It was reported that just three days later, chiefs from twenty-nine nearby villages assembled to greet Menéndez and his men and possibly to provide advice to Chief Tocobaga. With them were more than 1,500 warriors who, according to archaeologist Jerald Milanich, "paraded before the Spaniards in a show of strength." Hungry for a skirmish, the Spanish soldiers were visibly overjoyed at the sight of the warriors. Ironically, their reaction was supposedly misread by the Tocobaga as one of friendship. Perhaps for this reason, the Tocobaga people gladly consented to a peace treaty with Carlos and the Spaniards. As part of the agreement, the Tocobaga also returned several Calusa prisoners to Carlos on the condition that the Spanish defend them should the Calusa later violate the treaty. According to historian John H. Hann, the Tocobaga's willingness to make peace under this stipulation suggests that they were weaker militarily than the rival Calusa. It is certainly possible that the Tocobaga entered the treaty with the Spanish only to ensure protection from their stronger, ambitious neighbors to the south.

The significance of what had occurred cannot be overstated. Although the Spanish had themselves entered into treaties with different indigenous groups throughout the Americas (or at the very least had managed to coexist with them), this may well have been the first instance of a European brokering a peace agreement between two different indigenous societies—a remarkable achievement, especially considering the animosity that the Calusa held toward the Tocobaga (and, presumably, vice versa).

Having achieved the treaty, Menéndez sailed away with Carlos and the Calusa warriors and released prisoners, leaving behind thirty soldiers commanded by Captain Garcia Martínez de Cos, who would continue searching for the alleged waterway across the peninsula, the existence of which the Tocobaga erroneously confirmed. Also remaining was a Jesuit priest, Father Juan de Rogel, who would attempt to convert the Tocobaga to Catholicism.

THE CONNECTION OF THESE EVENTS TO THE CITY OF SAFETY HARBOR

Archaeologists have been unable to positively identify the site where this peace treaty was negotiated and entered, the village that Menéndez referred to as "Tocobaga." It was reported, however, that these events occurred at the principal settlement of the Tocobaga people. Given the evident size of the settlement that existed in today's Philippe Park and its strategic location on a bluff overlooking Tampa Bay, it is believed that this was the village most likely visited by Menéndez and the Calusa in 1567.

Although the city currently does not exhibit any historic markers commemorating these events, residents of Safety Harbor have long held this belief with civic pride. In 1966 or 1967, the city performed a dramatic reenactment of this event, coinciding roughly with the 400th anniversary of the treaty.

Over the years, a number of Spanish artifacts have been discovered in the park dating from the mid-sixteenth century, which lends credence to this notion. It is impossible to tell, however, whether these artifacts came from an earlier expedition (such as the mission of Fray Cancer) or were acquired through trade with other nearby villages. Still, in 1900, a surveyor named Captain John Walton allegedly found remnants of Spanish fortifications in Philippe Park, which, if true, would almost certainly confirm this theory. This claim cannot be proven, however, and one wonders how an early Florida pioneer would have the expertise to identify the remains of Spanish-built structures from a much earlier era or differentiate the remains from, for example, the destroyed home of an earlier settler or a temporary fishing camp.

The Aftermath of the Calusa-Tocobaga Treaty

The Spanish garrison at Tocobaga would last for less than a year. When Father Rogel returned with additional supplies after a trip away, he found the Indian village deserted and all of the soldiers dead. Outraged, and unable to find anyone to punish, the Spanish soldiers accompanying him burned the village. Father Rogel later blamed the tragedy on the behavior exhibited by the Spanish soldiers, claiming that they had demanded food, beaten and killed the Tocobaga and even abused the women. The Tocobaga, he maintained, had finally had enough of such "overbearing, cruel, and harsh" treatment and rose up against the Spanish.

The fort and mission constructed in Calusa territory would not be successful for much longer. Carlos remained furious with Menéndez for choosing to negotiate a peace treaty over helping him make war against the Tocobaga. After their return from Tocobaga territory, hostilities eventually erupted between the Spanish and Calusa, and the Spanish soldiers killed Carlos and other members of the Calusa tribe before abandoning the fort and mission in 1569.

Periodically, the Spanish continued to have contact with the Calusa. In 1614, Spanish forces attacked the Calusa as part of a war between the Calusa and Spanish-allied tribes around Tampa Bay. A Spanish expedition to ransom captives held by the Calusa in 1680 was forced to turn back; neighboring tribes refused to guide the Spanish for fear of retaliation. In 1697, Franciscan missionaries established a mission to the Calusa but abandoned the post after a few months. The Calusa, however, continued to thrive. It is believed that they did not entirely vanish from Florida until the mid-eighteenth century, primarily as a result of exposure to smallpox and other diseases. Violence with other groups might have also contributed to their diminishing numbers. Some may have migrated to Cuba between 1711 and 1761.

Although brief contact by messengers and soldiers occurred in the early part of the seventeenth century, this was the last major attempt by Spanish explorers and missionaries to interact with the Tocobaga in the Tampa Bay region.

There were few further European excursions to Tampa Bay during the coming decades. In the eighteenth century, the British made no effort to settle the central Gulf Coast during their brief control of Florida. In 1793, a trading post was established on the eastern shore of Tampa Bay by Captain Vicente Folch y Juan, who would later become the Spanish governor of

Doomsday. Original painting by Stuart Dvork.

West Florida, but it was manned for less than a year before the soldiers and merchants were transferred north to protect against encroaching English and French forces. With the possible exception of transient fishermen from Cuba, more than two centuries would pass before another nonnative would set foot on the Pinellas peninsula.

The Tocobaga themselves would not survive that long. By the early or middle part of the eighteenth century they were all gone, leaving behind only large earthen mounds littered with artifacts, shells and human remains. Their history is the subject of the next chapter.

Chapter 4

THE TOCOBAGA PEOPLE OF
SAFETY HARBOR

B efore the arrival of the Spanish explorers and missionaries, American Indians had already been living on the central west coast of the Florida peninsula for centuries. Indeed, archaeological evidence indicates that the first indigenous people came to this area between twelve and fifteen thousand years ago. Back then, environmental conditions were much different than they are today. The climate was cooler and drier, and now-extinct animals such as the mammoth, ground sloth and saber-tooth tiger roamed among oak and hardwood forests. The sea level was lower, and the shoreline extended as much as fifty miles into the Gulf of Mexico. Tampa Bay was dry land.

The people of that era were nomadic, following the seasonal availability of plants and the migratory paths of large mammals. In addition to providing food, the mammals were relied on for clothing, material for shelters and tools made from bone. Not much is known about these people. Some archaeological evidence of their presence in Florida, such as arrow and spear points, has been found along rivers. Due to the receding shoreline, however, many prehistoric sites from this period are now likely under water and cannot be examined.

Over time, the climate gradually changed. Pine forests replaced the hardwood forests and savannas. The Ice Age mammals died out. Tampa Bay filled with water. Adjusting to these new conditions, the early Floridians eventually settled in permanent sites on the coasts or near rivers. They also began hunting smaller game like deer, raccoon and opossum and relying more on wild plants, fish and shellfish for food. Evidence of these people has been found in Safety Harbor. In 2008, a spear point believed to be between six and eight thousand years old was discovered in Marshall Street Park. A year later, an eight-year-old boy unearthed a five-thousand-year-old point.

After the passage of several successive eras that were marked primarily by the development of tools, different types of ceramics and changes to burial rituals, a new culture was formed by the prehistoric people of the central Gulf Coast around the year AD 900. This society lived near the water in an area concentrated around Tampa Bay and relied heavily on seafood, most notably shellfish. Unlike the earlier Floridians, this culture left behind substantial archaeological evidence of its existence. Sites have been discovered throughout Sarasota, Manatee, Hillsborough and Pinellas Counties, but the most extensive was unearthed in Safety Harbor's Philippe Park and its surrounding area. In recognition of the significance of these ruins, anthropologists refer to this developmental phase simply as the "Safety Harbor period" or the "Safety Harbor phase" and to the people as the "Safety Harbor culture." The Safety Harbor culture included a number of distinct indigenous groups encountered by the Spanish explorers and missionaries in the sixteenth century, among them the Ucita, Mocoso and Pojoy. The relative strength and influence of each of these individual groups probably varied as leadership and population changed over successive generations. But by the 1560s, the most prominent group of peoples among the Safety Harbor culture was unquestionably the one visited by Pedro Menéndez de Avilés: the Tocobaga.[3]

About the Tocobaga

The Tocobaga may be rightfully considered the first permanent residents of Safety Harbor. Unfortunately, little is known about Tocobaga society, providing an incomplete picture of what must have been a fascinating,

3. The Tocobaga may not have been as strong earlier in the century. Contact with the Spanish explorers of the early sixteenth century such as Hernando de Soto might have negatively impacted the populations of some of these other groups through disease and violence. If true, this may have been the impetus that allowed the Tocobaga to increase the scope of their influence by the time of Menéndez's visit.

vibrant culture.[4] Other than archaeological excavations, most available information comes from sparse accounts written by Spanish explorers, missionaries and prisoners during the mid-sixteenth century. The Spanish were not completely unbiased observers, however, and it must be remembered that they may have been guilty of framing Tocobaga culture in relation to European society, economy, morals and industrial development of the time, as well as through the prism of their own attitudes and agenda toward the indigenous population.

The most intriguing account was written by a Spanish sailor named Hernando de Escalante Fontaneda, who, as a thirteen-year-old boy in the late 1540s, was shipwrecked on the Gulf Coast of the Florida peninsula. He then spent approximately seventeen years living among the Calusa and various other tribes in southwest Florida. After being rescued (possibly freed by the Calusa as a sign of goodwill when Menéndez de Avilés first visited in 1566), Fontaneda penned a short memoir depicting the indigenous people he had encountered, including the Tocobaga. In addition, several members of the de Soto expedition (including de Soto himself) wrote about their experiences in varying amounts of detail, including their stay at the Indian settlement of Ucita upon first making landfall.[5] As discussed in Chapter 1, historians are

4. Moreover, some information widely reported about the Tocobaga is erroneous. A portion of what is recounted about their society is drawn from an essay written in 1978 by archaeologist Ripley Bullen entitled "Tocobaga Indians and the Safety Harbor Culture," which appears in the book *Tacachale: Essays on the Indians of Florida and Southeastern Georgia during the Historic Period*. Among other things, this essay expressed the view that Tocobaga society was divided into four distinct social classes: chiefs, also known as caciques; headmen; warriors and ordinary people; and slaves, who may have been shipwrecked Europeans or captured Indians from other cultures. In a private communication with one of the authors, Jerald Milanich, the curator emeritus of archaeology of the Florida Museum of Natural History and a recognized authority on the American Indians of Florida (as well as the editor of *Tacachale*), explained that Bullen mistakenly believed that the Tocobaga and other Tampa Bay Indians were a branch of a group of American Indians from northeast and north-central Florida called the Timucuans, "and he applied Timucuan social organization to the Tocobaga." Although more recent scholarship has reversed that thinking, the information contained in Bullen's essay continues to be quoted and cited in documents and other sources describing Tocobaga society.
5. Also providing information about the Tocobaga was the brother-in-law of Menéndez de Avilés, Gonzalo Solís de Merás, who accompanied the peace mission to Tocobaga in 1567 as Menéndez's chronicler. Father Rogel, the Jesuit priest left behind at the garrison, recorded his observations as well.

unable to pinpoint the precise location of this village. Regardless of where de Soto landed, however, both Ucita and another nearby village said to have been visited by de Soto called Mocoso would have almost certainly been situated within the limits of the Safety Harbor culture area, and as such, their customs and practices were likely to have been similar (if not identical) to those of the Tocobaga. This theory is supported by the fact that these descriptions of Ucita are consistent with archaeological remains of typical Tocobaga villages. Moreover, at the time Menéndez de Avilés negotiated the Calusa-Tocobaga peace treaty in 1567, both Ucita and Mocoso were quite possibly individual chiefdoms contained within the Tocobaga hegemony. For these reasons, the observations of Ucita and Mocoso by the members of the de Soto expedition have been incorporated into the summary of the Tocobaga culture that follows.

The Tocobaga of the mid-sixteenth century were organized as a loose collection of semi-independent clans or chiefdoms. At the time of Menéndez's visit, they were ruled by a supreme chief who lived in their principal town, also called Tocobaga. Outlying villages were ruled by their own sub-chiefs and frequently fought against one another. Often, chiefs married the sisters of other chiefs. They communicated among themselves using smoke signals. In total, there were most likely several thousand Tocobaga.

Marine resources constituted a major part of the Tocobaga diet. They ate fish, shellfish, turtles and an aquatic plant called watercress, as well as small mammals and deer. Unlike many of the people of west-central Florida, the Tocobaga also practiced a small amount of agriculture, growing pumpkins, beans and possibly even some maize.

The Tocobaga hunted with long bows and arrows that were "made of certain reeds like canes, very heavy and so tough that a sharpened cane passes through a shield." Some arrows were pointed, with the bones of fish as arrowheads. These were described as "sharp and like a chisel," which could have been fabricated from the spine of a stingray. Other Tocobaga arrows had sharp stone points "like the point of diamond," which could have been the arrowhead type known as a "Pinellas point." A second type of arrowhead sometimes located at Tocobaga sites is known among collectors as a "Safety Harbor point," which exhibits a triangular shape with a concave and sometimes flared base.

The de Soto chroniclers described the Tocobaga as master archers. It was said that they had the ability to fire three or four arrows in the time it took a Spanish crossbowman to release a single shot—and they seldom missed. Their tactics were difficult for the Spanish soldiers to counteract,

too. Summarized historian John H. Hann, "The Indians ran about with such agility that neither the crossbowmen nor the harquebusiers could aim at them effectively."

No description exists of the clothing worn by the Tocobaga, but some information about their appearance was recorded by members of the de Soto expedition when they encountered the Spaniard Juan Ortiz and a small number of the Mocoso people. It was noted that the Mocoso "were painted red [with a] certain ointment that the Indians put on when they were going to war or wished to make a fine appearance" and wore "many plumes," presumably in their hair or on their heads. For his part, Ortiz was described as having his arms tattooed "after the manner of the Indians," although this might have been a custom of the nearby Timucua that was practiced by the Mocoso and no other people of the region. They also strung pearls together like beads, which they wore around the neck or upper arms.

Like some other indigenous cultures of that era in the southeastern United States, Tocobaga settlements were characterized by the presence of large mounds constructed primarily of earth and sand. The most prominent of these would have a rectangular shape and a flat top and usually incorporated a ramp that led up the middle of one of its longer sides. This mound served as a supporting platform for a temple, where it is believed that bodies were cleaned and stored for later burial; thus, it is often called the village "temple mound." Also constructed on top of this mound were anywhere between a half dozen to twenty houses for the chief, his family and servants. The village of Ucita, for example, was described as consisting of seven or eight houses erected on a high hill near the beach, with the other houses located in the middle of the town. These structures were made of wood and covered with palm leaves, reeds or brush and decorated with carved wooden ornaments.

No one knows why the Tocobaga chiefs and their families constructed their homes on top of these artificial hills. It could have been done for safety from wild animals or enemies or for protection from flooding. Maybe the mounds were used to allow the Tocobaga people to see a farther distance along the bay. Perhaps part of the reason was comfort: twenty feet above ground level, the wind picks up, and there are fewer mosquitoes in the summertime.

At least some of their homes were large communal dwellings. In Ucita, de Soto had these structures destroyed in order to construct smaller houses

Opposite: Morning Hunt—Tocobaga. A Tocobaga tribesman stalks his prey in the misty morning hours. *Original painting and description by Theodore Morris.*

designed for three or four men each. At one village, the earlier Narváez expedition reported the existence of a house large enough to hold three hundred people, although the remaining structures of that village were described as being small. Unfortunately, excavations performed at village sites have failed to identify the outlines of a single house, so the size of Tocobaga buildings cannot be proven.

In addition to this great temple mound, the Tocobaga villages also included a smaller burial mound, which held ceramics and the remains of the dead. At Ucita, the burial mound featured a carved wooden fowl "with gilded eyes." Burial customs appear to have been an important part of Tocobaga society. It is believed that when Tocobaga people died, their bodies were placed in the temple, possibly stored in wooden chests above ground, like tombs. When Juan Ortiz was captured by the Ucitans, he was temporarily assigned the task of protecting the exposed bodies during the night from wolves and other predators. Once a year, a mass burial was held when the remains of all who had died during the previous year were placed in the burial mound and covered up to a depth of perhaps three or four feet. It has been reported that the Tocobaga treated this as a feast day. Fontaneda, the young shipwreck survivor, also recorded the following ritual:

> *When one of the principal cacique dies they cut him into pieces and boil him in some large jars, and they boil him two days until the meat separates from the bones, and they take the bones and join one bone with another until they put the man together as he was and put him in a house which they have for a temple. While they finish putting him together they fast four days. At the end of the four days, all the Indian town comes together and comes forth with him to the procession and enclose him, making much reverence, and then they say that all those who go to the procession gain indulgences.*

Tocobaga settlements also included irregularly shaped garbage and shell mounds called middens. Essentially garbage heaps, middens were often constructed of sand and shell and incorporated a wide range of items and artifacts such as animal and shell food refuse, bones, antler tools and ornaments, pottery fragments, stone tools and debris, features such as hearths, roasting pits, storage pits, post molds and living floors and sometimes even human remains.

Often, a pit is found nearby from which material was obtained to build these mounds. The area between all these structures was left as an open plaza, around which lived the members of the community. The plaza was kept free of garbage.

The End of the Tocobaga

Initially, introduction to Europeans seems to have had very little effect on the Tocobaga people. The Spanish did not stay long, and the forts and missions they left behind at the village of Tocobaga and the nearby Calusa capital of Calus were soon destroyed by these indigenous groups. It is unknown how long de Soto's encampment at Ucita lasted, but it is believed to have been located on the east side of Tampa Bay far from the Tocobaga. Over time, however, due to exposure to European diseases and repeated conflicts, the Tocobaga population began to decline until they vanished completely. The fate of the final Tocobaga people remains unknown. In 1677, a Tocobaga settlement was discovered near Tallahassee, but when or why migration occurred is also unknown. In the beginning of the eighteenth century, remnants of the tribe might have joined the Cuban-Spanish fishermen who were active in the area. Another theory is that the last of the Tocobaga might have merged with the Creek peoples moving southward into peninsular Florida. The Tocobaga sites were abandoned, although they may have been later occupied by Cuban fishermen in the eighteenth and nineteenth centuries when they established seasonal fish camps along the coast to catch mullet for sale in Havana.

Archaeological Excavations of Tocobaga Sites in Safety Harbor

Over the years, a great deal of archaeological evidence of the Tocobaga culture has been discovered in Safety Harbor. Small fragments of pottery and flint have been found along the surface or during routine land development surveys. The most significant discoveries were made during organized professional excavations at the Tocobaga village in Philippe Park, known by archaeologists simply as the "Safety Harbor Site."

Because of its size, historians generally believe this site to be the former Tocobaga capital. It is also the likely location of their village visited by Pedro Menéndez in 1567, as well as near to where he established a small garrison before it was destroyed several months later. As mentioned earlier, in 1900, a surveyor named Captain John Walton supposedly unearthed remnants of Spanish fortifications elsewhere in Philippe Park, which would seem to support this connection, but there is no evidence that this actually occurred.

The Tocobaga temple mound as it exists in Philippe Park today. *Photo by Warren Firschein.*

In any event, many European artifacts from that time have been discovered at the site, including an iron axe and silver tubular beads, lending credence to the idea that this was the village visited by Menéndez. However, such items could also have been obtained through trade.

The most visible feature of the Safety Harbor Site is the large, flat-topped, rectangular mound, which stands on a point of land protruding into Old Tampa Bay. Consistent with historic descriptions of other Tocobaga sites, this mound was likely once an artificial platform used for a temple and other structures. Currently, the mound measures about 150 feet in diameter and 20 to 25 feet high and levels off into a flat platform that measures about 100 by 50 feet. As a result of erosion, the mound is smaller today than when it was built. In 1978, a seawall was constructed in the hopes of preventing further destruction.

At one time, as was the case with other Tocobaga settlements, the site also included a burial mound located northwest of the temple mound. However, this feature was destroyed at some point after being excavated in 1930. A picnic shelter and playground now stand on or near the spot where this mound was most likely located. When it existed, the burial mound was said to be approximately eighty feet in diameter and ten to twelve feet high. Village debris was discovered between the large temple mound and the burial mound and stretching to the southwest at roughly a ninety-degree angle, forming an inverted "L" shape. The short end of the "L" extends out at roughly the same angle as the ramp leading up the side of the temple mound, implying that this area was used as a promenade or gathering place.

Allegedly, the first house of pioneer Odet Philippe (who is addressed in the next chapter) stood near the shore, just south of the large temple mound. After his home was destroyed in the hurricane of 1848, he resettled on a site slightly southwest of the mound, farther from the water. Supposedly, this house burned down many years later. No remains of this structure exist today, and its exact location is unknown. An examination of the area, however, reveals a flat, open field on high ground directly west and southwest of the mound. The southernmost edge of this field provides a beautiful view of the bay before the ground begins to slope downward toward the shoreline, and it is here that Philippe's second home was more than likely situated.

EXAMINATION AND EXCAVATIONS OF THE SAFETY HARBOR SITE

Although its existence was well known to archaeologists, the Safety Harbor Site was not excavated until 1930, a year after permission was granted by the landowner at the time, Thomas Palmer. Palmer, a local attorney, had resisted previous calls to excavate the site.

The dig was led by a young ethnologist named Dr. Matthew W. Stirling, who arrived with unimpeachable credibility and expertise. He had previously excavated the site on Weedon Island, and in 1925, he led an expedition to New Guinea, where he collected natural history specimens that remain on display at the Smithsonian Institution. In 1928, at the age of thirty-two, he was named the chief of the Smithsonian Institution's Bureau of American Ethnology. Later in his career, he would make significant discoveries about the Olmecs, considered the first major civilization in Mexico. In all likelihood, it was Stirling's credentials that convinced Palmer to finally allow access to his property.

With the help of his brother Gene, Dr. Stirling excavated the now-destroyed burial mound, which yielded a huge amount of human remains. The *Safety Harbor Herald* reported that an average of 20 skeletons were unearthed on a daily basis. Over 1,400 skeletons were found in total. The bones revealed that the residents of this village were a large, lean, muscular people. One interesting discovery was that the teeth of these skulls were apparently all found to be in perfect condition, without any sign of decay.

Examples of Tocobaga pottery on display at the Safety Harbor Museum and Cultural Center. *Photo by Warren Firschein.*

The bones uncovered by this excavation were allegedly taken by local farmers to be ground up and used for fertilizer.

Stirling also unearthed a large amount of pottery, mainly from the base of the mound near its edge. This style of pottery, which is often found at Tocobaga archaeological sites, is now known as "Safety Harbor Incised." These ceramics are not highly regarded and are described as generally poorly made and decorated. According to distinguished archaeologist Gordon R. Willey, who produced a landmark work on the archaeology of the American Indian cultures of Florida's Gulf Coast, "Shapes tend to be badly formed and designs vaguely conceived and executed with carelessness...The total feeling is one of break-down in the ceramic art, carrying with it the implications of an impoverishment of the cultural forces and traditions that served as an incentive and guide to the aboriginal pottery maker." Interestingly, many of the vessels found by Stirling contained intentionally made holes, suggesting that they had been destroyed as part of a ceremony or ritual.

In addition to the bones and pottery, Stirling also discovered some Spanish artifacts dating from the sixteenth century, including an iron axe with a curving blade and European pipe bowls, which appeared to suggest that this village was once visited by European explorers. This garnered immediate attention from the press. The headline on the *St. Petersburg Evening Independent* of March 15, 1930, dramatically proclaimed, "Smithsonian Excavators Find Proof of Spanish Exploration in Pinellas Indian Burial Mound," complete with photographs of skulls and bones from the dig. We can only imagine how the city's residents must have been riveted by the progress of this excavation. Many of the artifacts recovered during this dig were sent to the Smithsonian.

After Thomas Palmer passed away in 1946, the site was purchased by Pinellas County. In 1948, additional excavations were performed under the direction of Ripley Bullen and John Griffin, two archaeologists of the Florida Park Service. Bullen and Griffin unearthed pottery produced by the Tocobaga, including large bowls and jars, as well as stone artifacts such as arrow points, knives, hammerstones and grinding stones. Bone pins were found that are believed to have been used as part of hair ornaments. They also recovered several more European artifacts, including the remnants of Spanish olive jars. Today, those artifacts are housed at the Florida State Museum and in private collections. In 1949, Bullen and Griffin returned to the site to debunk claims by two county residents that a "vast treasure" lay buried inside the temple mound.

The most recent excavations were performed in the late 1960s by members of the Safety Harbor Area Historical Society and another group known as The Searchers. As before, tools, arrowheads, Tocobaga pottery shards and Spanish pottery from the sixteenth century were unearthed.

The site was designated a Registered National Historic Landmark by the U.S. Department of the Interior National Park Service in 1966. Today, the mound is surrounded by several large picnic shelters, and from ground level, it appears to be little more than a large hill covered with grass and vegetation. Visitors can climb up the mound using a paved walkway or a stone staircase that winds up the east side of the mound, where they can enjoy an excellent view of Tampa Bay.

THE LOVER'S OAK AND PIPKIN CEREMONIAL MOUNDS

In addition to the mounds in Philippe Park, there were once two other mounds in Safety Harbor: the Lover's Oak shell mound and the Pipkin ceremonial mound.

The Lover's Oak shell mound was given its name due to its proximity to the Lover's Oak tree, which marked the mound's southern end. This mound was considered to be the most southern element of the Tocobaga settlement in Safety Harbor and, from there, provided easy access to both Tampa Bay to the east and Alligator Creek to the south.

The shell mound was located near the Lover's Oak tree, where couples enjoyed picnics and also carved their initials in the bark. *Photo courtesy of Heritage Village Archives and Library.*

In approximately 1905, this mound was destroyed when the shells within it were removed for use on county roads. The mound was reported to be of oblong shape, about 300 feet long and 150 feet wide. From surviving images, it appears as though the mound was approximately twenty feet high.

However, the Lover's Oak tree still stands a few blocks south of the Safety Harbor Museum and Cultural Center, in the front yard of the Lover's Oak condominium complex. The tree served as a favorite meeting place for young people and picnic groups from the 1890s to the 1950s and was sometimes used as the site for a community-wide picnic.

The Pipkin mound was located on the property of D.M. Pipkin, just north of where the Safety Harbor Public Library currently sits. As was the case with the Lover's Oak mound, the Pipkin mound was destroyed years ago when the shell fragments within the mound were removed for use on local streets. A large oak tree grew on top of the mound. This tree, which still lives, is estimated to be approximately two hundred years old. Destruction of the mound underneath the tree created a large gap through the tangle of wide roots where they were once underground. It is known as the "elf tree."

✦ PART II ✦
THE PIONEERS AND EARLY SETTLERS OF GREEN SPRINGS

Chapter 5

ODET PHILIPPE

THE FIRST PIONEER

Few men who have lived on this old earth have encountered more thrilling adventures, more disheartening disasters than did Count Odette [sic] Philippe and none faced his adversaries more courageously.
—*D.B. McKay*

M ore so than any other person, Odet Philippe can stake a claim as the founding father of Safety Harbor. Widely acknowledged as the first nonnative person to permanently settle in Pinellas County, Philippe is credited with introducing grapefruit to Florida and is recognized as the first cigar maker in Tampa, a community ultimately known as the "Cigar City." At his plantation called St. Helena, located in what is now known as Philippe Park, he cultivated citrus groves that were once a popular tourist attraction. There, he successfully grew grapefruit from seeds and developed a particular method of budding and grafting to enhance his citrus crop. He is believed to be the first to plant grapefruit in rows. For these reasons, he may be the person most responsible for the growth of the citrus industry in Pinellas County.

Philippe's familial legacy is pronounced as well. The first nonnative child born in Pinellas County is believed to have been the son of Philippe's fourth daughter, Melanie. His descendants would marry into other prominent settler families in the area and become major figures themselves in the history of the region. Even today, his descendants populate the county.

Taken together, these facts mark Philippe as "a seminal figure in the history of peninsular Florida, and a primary figure in the development of Tampa

Portrait of Odet Philippe (circa 1787–1869). *Original painting by Jon Houglum.*

Bay," as biographer J. Allison Defoor maintained. But in addition to this list of accomplishments, Philippe's life contained many outlandish episodes that have reached near-legendary status. Like most good stories, though, the tales surrounding Odet Philippe are part fact and part fiction—and at times it is difficult to separate one from the other.

The Legend and Truth Behind Philippe's Early Life

According to various sources, Philippe was raised in Lyon, France, a nephew of Louis XVI, king of France until he was executed during the French Revolution in 1793. While in school, Philippe befriended the future emperor of France, Napoleon Bonaparte. Although Napoleon specialized in military history and strategy, Philippe focused on the study of medicine.

After Philippe completed medical school and became a surgeon, Napoleon appointed him to a position of high rank in the French navy—its chief surgeon, according to some. His service was exemplary; during a naval battle on August 26, 1804, Philippe so distinguished himself with his bravery that he was later awarded a special medal by Napoleon bearing the Philippe family coat of arms.

Just a few months later, however, Philippe's luck ran out, and he was captured by the British fleet at the Battle of Trafalgar. Philippe was brought to London as a prisoner of war and was eventually transferred to the Bahama Islands, at that time a British colony. There, after treating the illnesses of local residents, he was eventually given his freedom on the condition that he never return to France or England. With his options limited, Philippe sailed for Charleston, South Carolina, to begin his life anew.

So goes the widely told legend of Odet Philippe's origins. An incredible story—but very little of it is likely to be true. For one thing, the dates do not seem to match up correctly. When Philippe later sought U.S. citizenship, he filed papers indicating that he was born in 1787, which would have made him just seventeen years old when he claimed to have been captured at Trafalgar as the chief surgeon of the entire French navy. That birth date would also appear to have made it impossible for Philippe to attend school with Napoleon, who was born in 1769, nearly twenty years earlier. Although Philippe is often referred to as a "count," there is no evidence that he was related to King Louis XVI. It has been reported that the earliest mention of this alleged relationship is believed to date from 1921.

Philippe's descendant and biographer J. Allison DeFoor II has suggested that Philippe may have spread these stories of his origins himself and surmises that Philippe could have come from the French colony of Saint-Domingue. This is certainly plausible. At the time when Philippe would have been a child, Saint-Domingue was experiencing significant social upheaval. In 1791, after black African slaves in Saint-Domingue revolted against French rule, white refugees began to flee to the United States, many bringing their African slaves with them. After slavery was abolished in Saint-Domingue in

1799, the revolt culminated with the defeat of French forces and the colony's declaration of independence as the Republic of Haiti in 1804. Perhaps Philippe came to the United States during the early 1790s as the child of a French landholder seeking safety. Based on a pair of letters written much later indicating that Philippe had dark skin, DeFoor has speculated that Philippe may have been one of a large group of well-educated landowners of mixed race who fled "to safer environments in the face of a paroxysm of violence" during the struggle for independence. If this theory is true, Philippe would hardly have been the first settler to embellish his past or invent an entirely new background for himself. Ultimately, historians may never know the facts.

Philippe's Early Life in Charleston and Florida

Regardless of Philippe's actual origins, records reflect that in approximately 1808 he moved to Charleston, South Carolina, where he eventually married and had four daughters. In Charleston, it is believed that Philippe soon established a lucrative medical practice and engaged in large-scale farming. This, too, might have been invented; city directories in 1819 and 1822 listed him simply as a "Segar maker on East Bay Street."

After a series of business setbacks, Philippe lost virtually all of his wealth and left Charleston with his family aboard a ship he had purchased, which he named the *Ney* after one of Napoleon's marshals. They settled in Fort Lauderdale, which was then known by the name of New River. Deciding to try his hand at growing citrus and other tropical fruits, Philippe sailed to the Bahamas and returned with various types of seeds. Soon he produced a large grove of citrus, mangoes, guavas and avocados. But Philippe's time at New River would not last long. When friendly Indians warned him of the imminent outbreak of the Second Seminole War, Philippe departed his home and took up residence in Key West, where he established one of the area's first cigar factories. Philippe would later bring these cigar-making skills with him to Tampa.

One well-known tale from Philippe's life during this period claims that while sailing in Florida waters, Philippe and his family were taken prisoner when the *Ney* was intercepted by a pirate named John Gomez. Upon learning that Philippe was a physician, however, Gomez asked Philippe to treat him and his crew, who were suffering from an illness or fever. After

Philippe provided assistance, in gratitude Gomez bestowed Philippe with a chest of treasure and a letter that would provide him with protection from other pirates.

The story of Philippe's encounter with pirates seems too fantastic to believe, but nonetheless, Philippe likely did know John Gomez, who was a notorious pirate and an extraordinary figure from early Florida history in his own right. In fact, during the period that Philippe and his family resided in Key West, Gomez apparently let them stay in his home. To this day, the building located at 304 Elizabeth Street is known as the Pirate House. It is speculated that while in Key West, Philippe conducted business with Gomez and other pirates, possibly fencing their stolen goods. If true, this would explain how Philippe left Charleston "virtually penniless" yet "nevertheless managed to accumulate substantial funds in a short period of time," as described by DeFoor.

Shortly thereafter, Philippe decided to leave Key West, possibly because local authorities had begun to investigate his questionable activities. Before departing, however, Gomez supposedly provided Philippe with a map of what the pirate described as "the most beautiful body of water in the world, with the possible exception of the bay of Naples": Old Tampa Bay. Perhaps heeding his friend's advice, Philippe set sail up Florida's west coast.

PHILIPPE'S LIFE IN TAMPA BAY

Philippe settled in Tampa near Fort Brooke, where his fortunes soon turned once more. At the conclusion of the Second Seminole War, Congress enacted legislation called the Armed Occupation Act of 1842, which provided willing settlers with up to 160 acres of land in parts of Florida free of charge, under certain conditions. Recognizing a good deal when he saw one, on November 1, 1842, Philippe filed a claim for the maximum 160 acres on the northwest bank of Old Tampa Bay adjacent to "Worth's Harbour," presumably named for General William J. Worth, commander of the army's forces in Florida based at Fort Brooke during the later stages of the Second Seminole War. He received his permit in January 1843.

Once there, Philippe established his homestead. Possibly to further the alleged connection between himself and Napoleon, he named his plantation St. Helena after the island on which the former emperor was exiled.

Using plants brought from the Bahamas, Philippe established a new citrus grove, which is credited as being the first in central Florida. He planted oranges, limes and a large citrus known as a pomelo, sometimes called "shaddock" after the captain who first brought its seed to Jamaica from the East Indies in 1696. At his new plantation Philippe also cultivated grapefruit, which is a hybrid between the pomelo and the sweet orange. Later, he added tangerines, sappadillos, mangoes, guavas, lemons and avocados. Philippe transported his fruit by boat to New Orleans, where oranges sold for three cents each.

In addition to growing citrus, Philippe tried his hand at a variety of other industries and small business ventures. He grew tobacco using seeds brought from Cuba and supplied the soldiers at Fort Brooke with vegetables and cattle. He also started a variety of businesses in Tampa, including an oyster bar and a tenpin alley. Furthermore, he owned a one-man cigar-making business and is recognized as the first cigar maker in the Tampa Bay area. There are also allegations that Philippe's most lucrative business was the illegal and secret importation of slaves, though this remains unproven.

Despite a lack of evidence that Philippe received any formal training as a physician, it is likely that he practiced simple frontier medicine during his time at St. Helena. In 1936, an article printed in the *St. Petersburg Times* credited Philippe with "administering to sick Indians who came to the mineral springs nearby to correct their ailments."

In 1848, Tampa Bay was hammered by a devastating hurricane, considered by many to be the most intense to ever hit the region up to the present day. Living near the water, Philippe was not spared. After several days of wind and pounding rain, he heard a loud roar and saw a huge wall of water rushing up the bay. Thinking fast, he climbed up the nearby Tocobaga mound with his family, where he had built a small structure he called his "summer house." There, they remained safe from the ensuing flood. His home and grove, however, were destroyed. Supposedly, the chest of jewels that Philippe had allegedly received from the pirate John Gomez was also washed away and lost.

After the disaster, Philippe rebuilt his home at St. Helena and replanted his citrus grove. The reputation of the grove grew to such an extent that it eventually became a prominent local tourist attraction. In 1857, for example, one visiting soldier from Fort Brooke described Philippe's plantation as being as pretty as he had ever seen, with the sides of the nearby Indian mound "completely covered with lime and orange trees."

Philippe was a complex man who defies easy categorization. It is known, for example, that he managed his groves and cigar-making business with the help of slave labor. Some sources have reported that he rescued his slaves from

Model of what Philippe's home is believed to have looked like, displayed at the Safety Harbor Museum and Cultural Center. *Photo by Warren Firschein.*

the hurricane of 1848 along with his own family, but his relationship with his servants may have gone much deeper. One researcher has discovered that in November 1858, two young boys listed as "belong[ing] to Mr. Philippe" were baptized in Tampa. The Baptismal Register describes their mother as "colored" and as one of Philippe's servants. This researcher theorizes that "[t]hese children may have belonged to him not only as slaves, but also as biological sons."

During the Civil War, Tampa Bay was blockaded by Federal troops, and it was not uncommon for Union soldiers to ransack property and steal food and animals from nearby settlers. Philippe, then probably in his seventies, was too old to adequately defend his property from these threats. Instead, he traveled inland with his family and other early settlers to what is now Pasco County where he farmed until peace was declared in 1865. He returned to his plantation, where he remained until his death a few years later in 1869.

He was inducted into the Florida Citrus Hall of Fame in 1963.

Philippe remains a romantic figure of the early development of Safety Harbor. He was described as "a person of joyous spirit, noted for his frankness and rugged constitution; a brilliant student, excelling in mathematics, geography, Latin, French, and Spanish...[who] also distinguished himself as

a promising artist, turning out student paintings, disclosing mature ability."
Near his grave in Philippe Park stands a historical marker that reads:

> *On this promontory Count Odet Philippe, a native of Lyon, France, and surgeon in the French armed forces under Napoleon Bonaparte settled in 1842, arriving at this point in his sailing vessel the Ney. In this area he established St. Helena, his plantation, and upon it he was the first to adapt the grapefruit to Florida culture.*
>
> *Here he raised a large family, many descendants of which now reside in Pinellas County. He pioneered in the development of this area and endowed this site with a history rich in colorful atmosphere. His remains are interred not far from this spot.*

Historians might never be able to confirm or disprove many details about Philippe's life. Parts of his past Philippe may well have embellished himself, possibly to conceal his true origins or to give himself greater credibility among other early settlers. Some of these stories may have been invented to entertain his grandson DeJoinville Booth, who would ride out to St. Helena with his grandfather in the years before Philippe died and spend hours listening to tales of Philippe's early life. The youngster "loved to remember what Grandpa told him." Later, these stories were passed on to DeJoinville's daughter, Gladys Ganley, who published them in a series of newspaper columns in the 1960s. Much of this "family history" was also published in the *Tampa Sunday Tribune* in 1921 by DeJoinville's sister-in-law, Mrs. George Booth, who may have gotten this information from the same source.

Ironically, though, Philippe's ultimate legacy to the development of the community was built on who he was and his citrus cultivation skills, not on who he pretended to be. "Whatever the truth," summed up *Tropical Breeze* contributor and author Patricia Pochurek, "he was a fabulous person, an adventurer, and a Florida pioneer who made a home in the wilderness and brought the citrus and cigar industry to the area."

Chapter 6

PHILIPPE'S LEGACY

Safety Harbor's Impact on the Citrus Industry

The actions of Odet Philippe had an enormous influence on the development of the citrus industry across the Pinellas peninsula. According to the Florida Citrus Hall of Fame, where he was inducted in 1963, Philippe "was known for sharing generously with his neighbors, and he often handed out budwood and instructions on how to convert wild sour orange tree [sic] into producers of sweet oranges." Through these efforts, other early settlers soon began to cultivate groves in the area. One of these settlers, James P. "Captain Jim" McMullen, is credited with developing wooden citrus crates to improve the packing and shipping process. This style of crate, or something like it, is still utilized today.

In 1892, using seeds from one of Philippe's trees, A.L. Duncan, manager of the Milwaukee Groves in Dunedin, created a variety of white-fleshed grapefruit for commercial distribution known as the "Duncan." The Duncan is described as a cold-hardy species that is able to withstand the unseasonable freezes that periodically decimate other citrus crops throughout Florida. The development of the Duncan helped establish grapefruit production as a profitable agricultural industry.

Once immensely popular, the Duncan is now rarely sold commercially due to the extreme number of seeds present in the fruit. Despite its seediness, many aficionados consider the Duncan to be the tastiest and sweetest variety of grapefruit. Today, the Duncan is most likely to be found growing in backyards throughout the Tampa Bay region. A popular seedless variety of white-fleshed grapefruit, known as the "Marsh," likely arose as a mutation from the Duncan and thus also has its roots in Safety Harbor.

By the turn of the century, citrus production was one of the staples of Safety Harbor's economy, as well as that of the entire region. Because the town lacked its own rail connection, farmers brought their fruit to Largo, the location of the closest station. It was reported that forty-five thousand boxes of fruit were shipped from Largo during 1901 alone.

During the "boom years" immediately prior to the Great Depression, the selling of oranges and grapefruit was the town's primary source of revenue. The local packing houses actively sought seasonal workers, on one occasion even releasing a public notice in the *Safety Harbor Herald* that "fruit will be at the [packing] house ready to start work on Monday" and touting that "[e]nough fruit is in sight to keep the house running full time till late in the spring." In 1929, just sixty years after Philippe's death, W.L. Straub described the magnitude of the citrus groves that then stretched across the county:

> *The orange, the lemon, the kumquat, the grapefruit and the tangerine are as much the beauty of the peninsula as the rarest natural growth of the semi-tropics, the palm, the live oak with its feathery mist of Spanish moss. And from Tarpon Springs on the north to the southern boundaries of St. Petersburg on the south the earliest people have planted and we have preserved the groves. We have multiplied them, perfected tree and fruit, until now the visiting motor car in the month of February speeds on through miles and miles of white bloom, green leaf, golden fruit all in one blaze of magical fertility and wealth.*

Government figures from the 1926–27 growing season cited by Straub indicate that Pinellas County contained 359,686 orange trees, with 264,335, or 73 percent, then bearing fruit, and 361,121 grapefruit trees, of which approximately 307,173, or 85 percent, were fruit-bearing. This made Pinellas County second in citrus production among Florida's sixty-seven counties despite being one of the state's smallest counties measured by area. At the time, it was estimated that these citrus trees had a combined net value of $5,608,910. Such was Philippe's impact on local industry.

But the city's influence on the citrus industry was not limited to the cultivation of groves. In 1937, for example, a resident named James Bristow was awarded two separate United States patents related to processes for preparing citrus for commercial sale. The first, Patent No. 2,072,022, was awarded in February for his proprietary method of improving the outer appearance of the fruit through the application and absorption of a coloring

Postcard of a worker picking oranges. *Courtesy of Safety Harbor Museum and Cultural Center.*

agent. The second, Patent No. 2,079,278, was assigned to Bristow less than three months later for his method of cleaning dirt and other accumulated matter from the exterior of fruits and vegetables without the use of a solvent such as water, oil or soap.

The citrus industry continued to play a prominent role in the local economy into the mid-twentieth century. The groves especially employed many African Americans for four or five months every year, beginning in January. "You didn't need any skills to work there," recalled William Blackshear. "You came there with a strong back and got a fruit bag, and got on a truck and went out to pick fruit." Others worked in the nearby packing plants, packing and boxing the fruit after it had been washed and loading the boxes into crates. One of the largest local employers was the Bilgore Canning Company, which produced canned citrus, as well as molasses and feed for stock. During the mid-1940s, it was estimated that Bilgore employed sixty people during the seasonal peak.

Once packed, the citrus was transported to the Safety Harbor railroad station, where it was loaded onto cars and shipped north for commercial distribution on a train locally known as the "fruit special." Throughout the peak season, an entire boxcar would be loaded each day from this location.

The smell of citrus lingered in the air throughout the city, and many remember that aroma vividly to this day. "Oh, the orange blossoms," Sandie

Front of a brochure from the Tangerine Shop in Safety Harbor listing prices of citrus from Humphries Groves. *Courtesy of Safety Harbor Museum and Cultural Center.*

Brasfield recently recalled. "You could smell the blossoms clean across town. It was all groves. Everything had a whole different smell. You just knew where you were." Added Judi Baker, "Safety Harbor always smelled like jasmine, orange blossoms and the bay. If you walk on a still night the smell is still there."

But being heavily reliant on one industry left the area vulnerable to unexpected economic crises. The citrus crop throughout the county and Florida witnessed occasional devastation due to weather and infestation. During the winter of 1894–95, for example, the so-called Great Freeze destroyed an estimated 90 percent of Florida's citrus industry, reducing statewide production from 5.5 million boxes of fruit to just 150,000. Later, in 1930, the Mediterranean fruit fly invaded Pinellas County, resulting in the closure of nearby packing plants. Due to changing tastes, the price of grapefruit plummeted to just eight cents a box by 1948, further damaging the financial viability of the industry.

The final straw was the freeze of 1962. The county's citrus crop was slow to rebound, and as one source summarized, "Land in the county was too valuable thereafter to replant with citrus trees." As a result, "[s]ubdivisions, commercial centers, and roads replaced former groves." In 2002, it was reported that just thirty-eight acres were still devoted to the commercial production of citrus throughout the county. Only a few years later, these groves were shut down and the land sold due to the outbreak of citrus canker. Now, a car dealership stands where that final grove was located at the intersection of Belleair Road and U.S. 19 in Clearwater.

A few isolated citrus trees still stand in Philippe Park, possibly a remnant of Philippe's original groves. For the most part, however, this part of the region's history is little more than a memory to longtime residents, reflected by the occasional fruit tree planted in a homeowner's yard. The only remaining part of the city's citrus industry still openly visible to visitors is the Sun Groves shop in the northern section of the city, which sells Florida-grown citrus on site and for nationwide delivery, as well as a wide selection of marmalade, juice and homemade ice cream.

Chapter 7

THE EARLY PIONEERS, 1842–1885

A ttracted primarily by the Armed Occupation Act of 1842 (the "Act"), a host of settlers soon followed Odet Philippe to the Pinellas peninsula. This act of Congress, which was enacted in the aftermath of the Second Seminole War as a way to encourage settlement of most of Florida, provided that heads of families or single men over eighteen years of age were eligible to claim up to 160 acres of land, free of charge, if they agreed to live on the site for five years, farm at least five acres and bear arms against Seminoles and runaway slaves. Twenty-four claims were made under this act for land in present-day Pinellas County. Until then, the few settlers in this part of Florida were actually squatters, who established homes wherever they wished. One such squatter was James P. "Captain Jim" McMullen, whose family and descendants would later populate much of the county and contribute greatly to its development.

The first settler to join Philippe near Worth's Harbor under the Act may have been William Nelson, a seaman and oysterman who filed a claim to his land on February 21, 1843, and received a permit approximately six months later. Nelson remained nearly a decade; in March 1852, he sold the land to a man named William Cooley, a merchant who is believed to have been an acquaintance of Philippe's from his days in New River and whose family had been killed at the outset of the Second Seminole War. Before coming to the area, Cooley was appointed the first postmaster in Homosassa, as well as the commissioner of fisheries for Hernando County. A local politician, Cooley would later serve three terms on the Tampa City Council.

The seven McMullen brothers. Standing from left to right: John Fain, David, Malcolm. Sitting from left to right: William, Thomas, James, Daniel. *Courtesy of Heritage Village Archives and Library.*

Others came, too. In all, twelve claims were filed in the immediate area. On June 30, 1843, George Sullivan received a permit for land on the narrow peninsula that juts down on the other side of Worth's Harbor, about a mile east of Odet Philippe's homestead in what is now Oldsmar. Around the same time, Hugh McCarty arrived and, according to one source, became Philippe's nearest neighbor. McCarty owned a wood yard three miles south of Safety Harbor at what is now the approach to the Courtney Campbell Causeway. Other settlers to file claims for land near Philippe's homestead under the Act included Frederick Tresca, George Forsythe, Samuel Bishop and the family of Thomas Stanfield, but whether these people actually settled on the land awarded them is unknown. Today, these names have mostly faded from memory.

A few years later, another settler arrived who is better remembered today: Richard Booth. While an early report listed Booth as an English sailor, a descendant claimed that he arrived in America from London when he was just three years old, with his family settling in the New York City area. According to that same source, Booth joined the U.S. Army at Watertown, New York, and was stationed at Fort Brooke in Tampa. In any event, in May 1847, at what might have been the end of his enlistment period, Booth married Philippe's fourth daughter, Melanie, who was called "Millie" by her family and friends. The couple moved into Philippe's home before Booth filed his own claim and built a home approximately two miles west of the bay, along what is now McMullen-Booth Road. Their son, Odet W. Booth, better known as "Keeter," was born on August 4, 1853, and is widely believed to be the first person of European descent born on the Pinellas peninsula, beating James McMullen's son John by approximately ten weeks.[6] Although the Booth family became some of the foremost settlers in the region, their role in the development of the area often went unheralded—"never wanting to have their name in the public eye, [despite being] so often the 'power behind' all progressive endeavors," according to descendant Gladys Ganley.

The first pioneers to settle within what would become the early city limits of Safety Harbor were J.D. Young and William Mobley, who came along in approximately 1853. In 1855, a man named Colonel William Bailey purchased the land where the Espiritu Santo Springs flowed, forever altering the path of Safety Harbor's history. Bailey's story is addressed in the next chapter.

James P. "Captain Jim" McMullen

Other than Odet Philippe, the most prominent pioneer to arrive in the region during the mid-nineteenth century was undoubtedly Civil War veteran James Parramore McMullen, eventually known simply as "Captain Jim."

James was born in Telfair County, Georgia, on June 11, 1823, and grew up in a large family that included six brothers and five sisters. Sick with tuberculosis, James left his home at the age of eighteen to protect his family from possible infection. He traveled south for approximately 250 to 300 miles, eventually settling at Rocky Point, a small piece of land on the eastern shore of Tampa Bay. After remaining there for a short time, he moved to the west side of the bay, near the current western end of the Courtney Campbell Causeway and the north end of the Bayside Bridge, an area eventually known as "Bay View" or shortened to "Bayview." According to one family story, he selected this site because of its ample vegetation and "strip of sandy white beach, lapped by blue green deep water." McMullen remained in Bay View for a relatively short period of time, subsisting on seafood and the abundant wildlife, coming in contact with few other people.

---

6. "Keeter" Booth was Richard and Melanie's third child. His older siblings, Ortancha and Richard, were both born in Tampa.

In 1842, due to the temperate climate and seclusion, his tuberculosis went into remission, and he temporarily returned home to Georgia. On the return trip, James met Elizabeth Campbell. The two were married on December 16, 1844, at a settlement called Melendez, which is located near present-day Brooksville in Hernando County. The couple remained in Melendez for several years and had three children there. But James never forgot about his time spent living along Tampa Bay, even telling his brothers that the Pinellas peninsula was "the closest thing to heaven that he could imagine."

By the late 1840s, James returned to the region with his new family, where he claimed land and settled near Worth's Harbor pursuant to the Armed Occupation Act. There, James built a small log cabin and planted groves. The McMullen family did not stay at this location for long, however. According to one story, James and his friend Richard Booth were camping along a spring in or near Safety Harbor when the notorious hurricane of 1848 approached. The pair survived by taking cover at a nearby Tocobaga mound, although the mound was partially destroyed by the storm. Some believe that this experience convinced him to move to a new log cabin farther inland, away from the water.

Much of James McMullen's life on the Pinellas peninsula was spent at this second log cabin, which was located several miles west of Safety Harbor. This building is still standing, the oldest remaining structure built in Pinellas County. After surviving a devastating fire in 1976, it was moved to Heritage Village in Largo, where it can be visited today.

The McMullen log cabin as it exists today. *Photo courtesy of Pinellas County Communications Department.*

By now, captivated by his descriptions of the area, James's brothers had begun to follow him to the region. One of his brothers may have occupied James's original cabin near Worth's Harbor after it had been abandoned, until it "simply rotted away." Another brother, David McMullen, moved to what would become Safety Harbor in late 1865 or early 1866.

During the Civil War, the McMullen brothers served the Confederacy. James was named a captain in 1861, serving under General J.M. Taylor at Clear Water Harbor. At around the same time, the Booth and McMullen families fled to an encampment north for better protection. From there, James (now known as Captain Jim) and the other men became members of the "cow brigade," which was tasked with raising and herding cattle northward to feed and clothe suffering Confederate forces, while the women took turns guarding the settlement. Odet Philippe, then in his mid-seventies and far too old to fight, stayed with them in the camp. They planted gardens to produce food. When it was safe to return, they drove their few remaining cattle home only to find their houses had been ransacked in their absence.

After the Civil War, Captain Jim gradually began to focus more of his efforts on the cultivation and sale of citrus. As mentioned previously, he is credited with developing wooden citrus crates in order to simplify the shipping process.

In the mid-1870s, Captain Jim and his sons developed Bay View into a small town a few miles southwest of what would become Safety Harbor and about a mile and a half south of his log cabin. There, he built a sawmill, a packing house and a two-story hotel, while his son Dan operated one of the settlement's two stores. In 1875, the Bay View post office opened, with Captain Jim serving as the first postmaster. Mail was brought from Tampa by horseback two or three times a week. At the time, this was the closest post office until the Safety Harbor branch was established in 1890.

When James McMullen passed away in 1895, he left behind an extensive number of direct descendants and relatives through different branches of his immediate family. By the early 1900s, his family and their descendants supposedly numbered over one thousand people in the west-central Florida area. When his brother Daniel died in 1908 he was said to have been survived by seven sons and two daughters, forty-six grandchildren and five great-grandchildren, for a total of sixty direct descendants.

SYLVAN ABBEY

As his family and those of the other nearby settlers grew, James McMullen felt that it was necessary to establish a school to educate the pioneer children. So, while on a trip to transport citrus out of Florida, he recruited a teacher reportedly named Mrs. Dudley and brought her and her young daughter back with him.

Initially, the students met in the attic of Captain Jim's sugarhouse, a log building that was originally built as a place to produce syrup from sugar cane. Ever industrious, he constructed benches and a teacher's desk for the school's use. As more children attended classes, however, McMullen recognized the need for an even larger school.

In 1853 or 1854, with the help of other family members and Richard Booth, James McMullen built a one-room log school with a chimney and fireplace on a piece of land east of his cabin, not far outside the early town limits. The exact location of this school is unknown, but in an article from the *Safety Harbor Herald* in 1942, it was described as just south of Sylvan Abbey Cemetery, which would place it east of U.S. Highway 19 and near or a little bit south of Sunset Point Road today. James decided to name the school after the first student, the teacher's daughter, a girl named Sylvan Abbey.

Eventually, a long wagon with a covered top was constructed to convey the area children to school. Driven by Louise Pearce, affectionately known as "Mrs. Pet," the vehicle had two bench seats down each side with a step at the back and was pulled by two large, beautiful red horses that had been rented to the county by a farmer. There were often between fifteen and twenty-five children on this "bus."

The early school building also served as the Sylvan Abbey church. After Sunday services, many family members and guests would gather at one of the nearby McMullen homes for dinner before commencing their long journey back to their homes in Clear Water or Largo.

Nearby, a parcel of land was used as a cemetery for the region's early settlers. Following the tradition of the time, it is likely that these graves were placed in or close to the churchyard, although, as stated above, the exact location of that structure remains unknown. Today, the pioneer cemetery is part of the Sylvan Abbey Memorial Park, which adopted the name of the log cabin school. The oldest graves belong to William Taylor, who died July 7, 1853; his wife, Lavinca, who died March 4, 1860; and Catherine, the wife of Daniel C. Whitehurst, who died on December 11, 1857. Many of the other early headstones can no longer be read.

Grave site of early pioneer William Taylor. *Photo by Warren Firschein.*

In 1881, James donated ten acres of land near his log home to be used as a grave site for his relatives and close friends. That cemetery, which is still known as the McMullen Cemetery, contains his grave as well as those of members of the McMullen, Booth and Belcher families. Richard Booth, however, is buried in the pioneer section of the Sylvan Abbey Memorial Park. In June 1999, the graves of James McMullen's parents, grandmother and two sisters were moved to this cemetery from Brooks County, Georgia. These are now the oldest graves present, although none of these individuals was an original settler of the area.

CONTACT WITH THE SEMINOLE INDIANS

During the mid-nineteenth century, the early settlers occasionally came in contact with the Seminole people. After the conclusion of the Second Seminole War in 1842, tribal members were permitted to remain on an informal reservation south of the Peace River under the terms of the verbal truce agreement. They did not stay there, however, instead roaming more or less as they pleased, leading to periodic clashes with the early pioneers. Conflicts continued to escalate until they led to the Third Seminole War, which lasted from 1855 to 1858. In 1856, Captain Richard Turner organized local residents into a militia that pledged to take up arms against any Seminole who encroached on homesteaded lands. James McMullen, among other early settlers of the Pinellas peninsula, served in one such company. After the war, most of the remaining Seminole were transported west, but some remained in the area, unbeknownst to the early settlers. In 1859, the early area residents were shocked when a group of Seminole men, women and children emerged from the woods near Alligator Creek, where they had been secretly living on fish and oysters. According to W.L. Straub, the pioneers "promptly hustled [them] out to join their own people down towards the Everglades."

CONDITIONS FACED BY THE EARLY PIONEERS

It is hard to envision what life was like for the early pioneers who first arrived on the Pinellas peninsula in the mid-nineteenth century. Accounts by early settlers paint a picture of difficult environmental conditions with few creature comforts—a rugged wilderness, without roads or wagon trails, that was covered with forests, thick shrubs, palmettos and tall grass. The heat in summertime was brutal. Snakes could be almost anywhere. Finding it difficult to grow the crops they were accustomed to, people lived off pickled beef, dried beef and fish, pork sausage, white and blood puddings, salted meat, garden vegetables and dairy products.

The early settlers raised cattle and hogs, which were permitted to roam freely over the land to find food for themselves. Production of beef was the primary industry of the region. Farming of vegetables such as potatoes and corn was a distant second.

With building materials and tools in short supply, the early pioneers constructed their homes using hand-hewn logs that were "chinked with mud and covered with hand-made clapboards or shingles." Roofs were thatched, often with palm fronds. Glass and screen windows were rare. Mosquitoes and other biting insects were constant annoyances.

Furniture was mostly homemade and simple. The use of homespun and plain clothing was so widespread that, as one early settler later recalled, "nobody could point the finger of ridicule at anybody else."

Moreover, the early settlers were isolated. Until 1858, there was no railroad anywhere in the entire state of Florida. The roads were nothing but sand trails that snaked through the forests, seemingly at random, wherever several vehicles had gone previously. After a strong rain, travel would be hazardous, for it was easy for buggies or wagons to get stuck in the sand. There were no bridges. The closest place of business, which included stores and trading posts, was across the bay in Tampa, described as "a mere village, small and scraggly enough."

Even something as simple as retrieving mail was difficult. The first area post office, in Clear Water Harbor, wasn't established until 1859 and temporarily closed shortly thereafter, until the conclusion of the Civil War. Until regular postal service was established the settlers were forced to travel to Tampa. At church, a person planning to go to Tampa in the coming days would be identified and appointed to collect the mail for the entire community. The decision to travel to Tampa was not made rashly. The trip was often made on foot or with oxen, and it typically took two days to go around the bay in each direction. A week or more might pass before the mail was finally distributed. Boats were sometimes used to make the trip, but the voyage was no quicker and was sometimes endangered by thunderstorms.

But pioneer life had its rewards, too. For the experienced hunter, game was easy to come by. Deer and turkey "were so common as to be sometimes nuisances to farmers." Wrote early settler John Bethel of the lands near St. Petersburg around the time of the Civil War:

> There were deer, bear, 'coons, 'possums, rabbits, squirrels, turkeys, geese, ducks, whooping cranes, blue and white cranes, curlew, quail, plover, snipe, etc. Besides these there were panthers and wildcats by the hundreds, and 'gators just as plentiful. All one had to do was to load his gun and go off from his enclosure, so as not to shoot any of his family, and kill a turkey or some other kind of game for dinner.

In addition to hunting, the early settlers fished in the lakes, gulf and bay with nets for myriad fish, including grouper, tarpon, snapper, amber jack and trout. Shellfish such as oysters, stone crabs and scallops were abundant, too. They collected turtle eggs and bird eggs from the beaches and shores.

All in all, it was not a terrible existence. While some settlers gave up and left, most stayed. And others kept arriving.

THE PIONEERS AND EARLY SETTLERS OF GREEN SPRINGS

POPULATION GROWTH DURING 1842–1880

Due in part to the Armed Occupation Act, the population surged throughout the Pinellas peninsula during the middle of the nineteenth century. Although the first (lawful) residents had arrived only in the early 1840s, the Pinellas peninsula already had 178 residents by 1850, according to that year's federal census.

The 1850s continued to see growth in the region's population. As was the case with Odet Philippe, some of these immigrants arrived from Key West. Most, however, were white farmers from throughout the southern United States, known as "crackers." Like James McMullen, many of the settlers who moved to the Pinellas peninsula during the 1850s had been living at the settlement of Melendez near Brooksville. Perhaps drawn by James's success and/or enthusiastic descriptions of the region, by 1860, more than a dozen of these families had settled in central and northern Pinellas.

By the Civil War, Hillsborough County (which included what would become Pinellas County) had a population of 2,417 whites and 564 enslaved blacks. At the time, estimates of the number of people who lived on the Pinellas peninsula ranged from 52 to 82 families containing 381 people.

Area growth tracked that of the rest of the state. Between 1850 and 1860, the statewide population increased by 60 percent to approximately 140,000 residents. Twenty years later, the generally accepted length of a single generation, the state's population was up to nearly 270,000, and approximately 240 households and 1,100 people resided on the Pinellas peninsula. Roughly 29 households had been established in the Safety Harbor area. An organized community was already starting to form.

Chapter 8

THE ESPIRITU SANTO SPRINGS

*Frequented by the Aborigines or Mound-Builders, as the Great Mound on the Bluff
hard by attests, then by the Historic Indian, the Spaniards, the Path-Finding Pioneers,
United States soldiers during the Indian Wars, the early settlers of South Florida,
and now by the Moderns, Citizens, and Tourists, each and all in their day and time
showing their appreciation of Espiritu Santo Springs by their annual pilgrimages to
this Ancient Mecca of Health, Pleasure, and Rejuvenation.
The Healing and Health-Giving Waters of these Famous Springs have cured
well-established cases of Paralysis, Eczema, Rheumatism, Dyspepsia, Gout,
Dropsy, Bright's Disease, Kidney, Bladder and Urinary Troubles (including
stone in the bladder), Stomach Complications of gravest character, Catarrh
of Head and Stomach, Blood Poison of Virulent Type, Nervous Prostration,
Chronic Dysentery, Fistula, Jaundice, Torpid Liver, Female Disorders, and
General Debility. For Stomach Trouble, Kidney, Bladder and Urinary Affections,
Dyspepsia, Indigestion, and Rheumatism the water may be considered a Specific,
acting gently, naturally, quickly and efficaciously. The medicinal virtues of these
Famous Waters have "healed many with divers diseases" in so short a time as to
appear marvelous. Many cured where all else failed.
—from a 1910 pamphlet promoting the Espiritu Santo Springs, presumably
written by Captain James F. Tucker*

From deep within the sand near the Tampa Bay shore, the Espiritu Santo
Springs bubble up to the surface. This unlimited, healthy source of fresh
water is undoubtedly what first attracted the Tocobaga people to the area.

They established their village a short distance north of the springs, on a strip of land strategically jutting out into Old Tampa Bay, providing easy access to both the natural mineral waters and abundant seafood.

Much later, the discovery of the Espiritu Santo Springs was credited to Hernando de Soto and his party in 1539, although no one can say with any certainty whether de Soto arrived at the springs or even traveled through the Pinellas peninsula at the start of his expedition through the southeastern United States. Regardless of whether they were visited by de Soto, the springs later played a vital role in the development of the growing community.

No one knows how the early pioneers of the nineteenth century first became aware of the existence of the natural mineral springs. Several myths have been passed down over the years. According to one story, when the region's first settler, Odet Philippe, treated the local American Indians during their illnesses, they repaid his kindness by telling him of the astonishing healing powers of the nearby springs.

Another version revolves around a colonel named William J. Bailey, who served at nearby Fort Brooke during the Second Seminole War. Allegedly, after a skirmish, an American Indian taken prisoner by Bailey and General William Harney told them "of the wonderful waters that were flowing forth from the sand that would cure all matter of ills." Bailey was intrigued by this story, and after the war was over, he went in search of these waters. Bailey eventually located the springs on the west shore of Old Tampa Bay and purchased the land from the U.S. government. A slight variation of this story insists that it was Colonel Bailey's father who had been told about their existence and that Bailey, remembering the stories told by his father, sought them out. In any event, it is established that in 1855, William Bailey Jr. purchased the land on which the springs flowed.

It seems odd that these fresh mineral springs were not purchased until 1855, perhaps twelve or thirteen years after Philippe established his plantation of St. Helena. Even if Philippe hadn't learned about the springs from local American Indians, surely the early settlers had discovered them on their own before then. According to one source, however, on May 15, 1843, a man named John Conrad Dalwig recorded a claim to land located "about one mile southeast of Worth Harbor, St. Helena, or Phillippiville, along Old Tampa Bay...including the Spring..." If true, this would appear to make Mr. Dalwig the first owner of the Espiritu Santo Springs. For reasons that have been lost, this land (if ever privately owned) eventually reverted back to the government, thereby allowing Bailey to purchase the property later.

For many years, the mineral springs were known as the Bailey Springs, or Bailey-by-the-Sea, and Colonel Bailey made them available for public use. Buoyed by claims that the mineral waters restored the health of the sick, the reputation of the springs grew. The most famous of these stories was that of Jesse D. Green, a farmer who allegedly visited the springs in 1870. When he arrived, Green had been paralyzed below the waist for four years. Although his physicians declared his condition incurable, upon hearing about the restorative properties of the mineral water, Green traveled to Florida from Georgia and purchased a small piece of property near the springs. According to local lore, he drank the water and bathed in it three times a day in a bathhouse built for his use. Within a year, Green "was plowing and hoeing in his orange grove near by, practically a well man."

The Espiritu Santo Springs remained in the Bailey family for over a half century. For a time, the resident physician supervising the facility was a man named Dr. J.T. Green. The similarity between Dr. Green's name and that of the invalid allegedly cured by the springs is suspicious, and it is certainly possible that the story about Jesse D. Green was invented to promote the health benefits of the mineral water. A history of Pinellas County written in 1929 seems to imply that they were the same person. Regardless, either on account of that "miraculous cure" or because of Dr. J.T. Green, around 1890, the community became known as Green Springs.

As time passed, the fame of the healing properties of the fountain at Green Springs increased. More and more people visited the springs. They bathed in a large swimming tank, as swimming pools were then called, that was built by Colonel Bailey and was filled by the overflow from the mineral springs. Some stayed in small houses that were offered for rent by the week or month on nearby land owned by a man named Captain Johnson, who is said to have purchased his property from Jesse Green. Each of the small houses was supplied with water from a small pump, while outhouses were located approximately fifty feet away. More often, visitors camped out in tents or erected palmetto thatched huts near the shore. As there were no stores, visitors either brought their own food or fished for mullet in the bay using nets.

The biggest nuisance was hogs, which were permitted to roam at will and liked to root under the houses to sleep. They would eat any food that was left outside. To cope with this problem, more experienced visitors would bring dogs with them to chase the hogs away.

In the early 1900s, Bailey's son-in-law, James F. Tucker, a former captain of the Confederacy during the Civil War, realized the commercial potential

Early bathers pose in front of the first buildings constructed over Espiritu Santo Springs. *Photo courtesy of Heritage Village Archives and Library.*

Early buildings at Espiritu Santo Springs and the adjacent swimming tank. *Photo courtesy of Heritage Village Archives and Library.*

of the property and converted the springs into a viable business. To better attract vacationers and those seeking treatment from the restorative waters, Tucker erected a pavilion around the already-existing swimming tank and made other improvements, such as installing pumps at the springs and enclosing them under a shelter. Dressing rooms were enlarged. He also had the water bottled for nationwide distribution.

In winter, when tourists arrived, the mineral water was too cold for many visitors to swim. Instead, they would slowly enter the water while grasping hold of the steps to immerse themselves for a short time. It was said that men and women bathed at separate times and wore old clothes for swim attire. Entry was free for those who needed treatment and couldn't pay, as well as for people described as "ministers of the Gospel."

Captain Tucker constructed a dock that supposedly extended a half mile or more into Old Tampa Bay, which was used both for the shipment of freight and as a debarkation point for visitors and tourists from Port Tampa until the Seaboard Railway was established in 1914. After that, the dock was apparently abandoned, at least with regard to commercial purposes.

When Captain Tucker died in 1913, his wife, the former Virginia Bailey, took over operation of the facility. In the meantime, the multiple springs were utilized by other ventures as well. In 1914, after discovering three different types of mineral water on his property northwest of Espiritu Santo Springs, resident Daniel M. Pipkin built a hotel and baths establishment, which he named the Pipkin Mineral Wells Hotel. Pipkin would host community picnics and fish fries on his property and would later provide mineral water to an adjacent health facility, Dr. Barth's Hotel & Baths.

The Tuckers' policy of providing spring water free of charge to those unable to pay ended in 1919, when U.S. government revenue officials required the Espiritu Santo Springs Co. to pay taxes on all mineral water taken away from the springs. In response, an admission fee was established at five cents a day, ten cents for those wishing to carry away a gallon of water. This appears to have continued until January 1927, when the *Safety Harbor Herald* reported that all visitors would once again be permitted to drink from the fountain without charge.

A SHORT DESCRIPTION OF THE SPRINGS

There were, and are, five separate fresh mineral springs in the area, each with its own individual chemical makeup and a slightly different taste. One of these springs appears to have been permitted to run freely and has never been utilized by the facilities. Over the years, the names of these springs have been changed, apparently for promotional reasons. The four utilized springs were initially referred to as the Bath House Spring, which was credited with curing Jesse Green; the Drinking Spring, the largest and most generally used; the Old Bath House Spring, said to be "found efficacious in all cutaneous diseases"; and the Beauty Spring, named so "because of the marked effect upon the skin in softening, cleansing, and beautifying." By 1966, the four operational springs had been renamed as De Soto, Phillippe, Baranoff and Santo. The name Baranoff would later play a part in the facility's history in the middle of the twentieth century and is discussed in Chapter 11. There is also a reference to the names Beauty Springs, Stomach Springs, Kidney Springs and Liver Springs, which reflected the purported health benefits of each source of water, although it is unclear when these names were utilized.

Today, visitors to the facility have an opportunity to taste water drawn from a combination of three of the springs. The water is bottled daily through a reverse osmosis process and, when drunk, leaves a slight but not unpleasant mineral aftertaste.

The pavilion and dock at Espiritu Santo Springs. *Photo courtesy of Heritage Village Archives and Library.*

Early Promotion of the Espiritu Santo Springs

During his time managing the operation of the facility, Captain Tucker actively promoted the health benefits of the mineral springs. The most notable of his advertising efforts is a seventy-five-page pamphlet written in 1910 that is quoted at the beginning of this chapter. The pamphlet prominently boasts that the springs were the original "Fountain of Perpetual Youth" sought by Ponce de León and ultimately discovered by Hernando de Soto in May 1539 and lists a number of additional claims about the springs, including:

That in point of discovery it is the oldest in America.
That in manifold cures of "divers disease" it is the most wonderful.
That it has cured many when all else failed.
That it has a wider range of cures than any spring yet discovered.
That its action is prompt and its benefit more speedily experienced.
That it is a specific in more diseases than any other known healing mineral water.
That as an alternative, energizer, restorative and normalizer it is without an equal.
That in female diseases it is most efficacious.
That it has a rejuvenating effect upon the old.
That it is a natural remedy for alcoholism and the drug habit when administered under the direction and discipline of a physician.
That in all functional diseases coming within its range great benefit, if not a complete cure, may be reasonably looked for, the most refractory cases often yielding to its curative and healing properties.
That in cases of organic disease the general health may be built up, life prolonged and made more comfortable.

Though these statements may seem incredible and a bit humorous today, the most astonishing claim was one made by Dr. J.T. Green himself. In a letter reproduced in the 1910 pamphlet, Dr. Green wrote, "I have often wondered why Espiritu Santo Springs water proves so efficacious in the treatment of certain diseases, and only until lately have I been enabled to demonstrate, by actual scientific tests, that they owe their efficacious condition to the fact that during their subterranean passage they flow over beds of pitch blends, and thereby become radio-active."

That's right: radioactive mineral water. To support Dr. Green's claim, the pamphlet cites a then-recent article in *McClure's* magazine that profiled Nobel Prize–winning scientists Marie and Pierre Curie and speculated

ESPIRITU SANTO SPRINGS,
(Springs of the Holy Spirit,)

On Old Tampa Bay, near Tampa, Fla.

These Famous Springs Boast of Being the Original
" Fountain of Perpetual Youth," Sought for
by Ponce de Leon, and Discovered
by Hernando De Soto in
May, 1539.

Espiritu Santo Springs

are in Point of Discovery the Oldest in America,
and in Manifold and Miraculous Cures
the Most Wonderful.

A. D. 1539—371ST ANNUAL SEASON—A. D. 1910.

After |Reading, Please Hand |to Your Sick
or Afflicted Friend.

FOR FURTHER INFORMATION, ADDRESS

ESPIRITU SANTO SPRINGS,
NEAR TAMPA, FLORIDA.

Cover of the 1910 pamphlet promoting the Espiritu Santo Springs. *Courtesy of Safety Harbor Museum and Cultural Center.*

that spring water with radioactive properties might hold significant health benefits when drunk. At the time, radium was widely considered without risk, as demonstrated by the experience of the U.S. Radium Corporation, which produced luminous paints between 1917 and 1926 until many of the factory workers developed symptoms of radioactivity poisoning, eventually leading to the enactment of several important labor safety standards and regulations.

But in the early 1900s, James Tucker ran with this idea. He wrote that "the peculiar sensation and marked exhilaration of the bath...would seem to indicate the presence of radium in unusually generous quantities in the waters of these already famous Springs." He referred to the springs as the "Espiritu Santo Springs Radio-Mineral Water" and touted the benefits of drinking and bathing in radium-infused water.

Thankfully, there is no support for this assertion. Over the years, the water from each of the individual springs has been analyzed a number of times and has been found to contain differing amounts of various ordinary minerals such as magnesium, iron, calcium and sodium chloride. No radium has been found.

TESTIMONIALS AND THE SALVATION OF GOLDIE BANKS

The 1910 pamphlet included thirty-five pages of testimonials attesting to the quality of the spring water and providing detailed descriptions of the various illnesses that were said to have been cured through its use. One man wrote, "I came here on crutches, with rheumatism, also stomach trouble. After five weeks I discarded the crutches, and left a new man." Others reported that the springs cured them of paralysis, blood poison, rheumatism, kidney trouble, stomach and liver troubles, indigestion and other illnesses or adverse physical conditions.

Of particular note are two testimonials relating the cures of young children. According to one:

> From infancy my baby had indigestion. It grew worse and worse, until her stomach became ulcerated and she could not retain any kind of food...After drinking [the spring water] four days my baby commenced to improve, and increased in weight from eight pounds to sixteen pounds within a few weeks. She is now two and one-half years old and is entirely well. I attribute it all to Espiritu Santo Springs water.

Another said:

> *My little grand-daughter, Helen Bustillo, at that time three years old, had suffered from the age of eight months, when she began to eat solid food, with stomach trouble and acute indigestion. This condition became chronic, and we had to be most careful of her diet, as almost everything disagreed with her…This low condition of health followed her until she was nearly three years old, when her physical condition was so badly reduced in flesh and strength, her stomach constantly swollen to nearly twice its normal size, that we became alarmed for her recovery…After arriving [at the springs], it was five days before we could persuade her to drink the water; then she began to drink, and soon learned to love it…Within a month we stopped all medicine, giving her the water only. After a six weeks' stay we considered the child cured. She had gained flesh, strength, color, and vitality, and her stomach had gone down to its normal size. This was about one year ago. She has been well ever since, and is now a picture of health, and has had no occasion for a physician in all that time. We are perfectly satisfied that this great improvement in her health and final cure was wrought by the waters of the Espiritu Santo Springs.*

The promotional campaign worked. The fame of the Espiritu Santo Springs spread and may in fact have saved at least one young life. In 1917, just a few years after this pamphlet was printed, an African American girl named Goldie Smith was born in rural Georgia. Goldie was possibly born prematurely; she recalls her mother, Amanda, telling her that "she could put me in a jar, with a lid on it, I was so small." According to Goldie, her father, Charley Smith, was told about the Espiritu Santo Springs and that "if he brought me to Florida to drink the spring water, I could gain weight." Fearful for her survival, in 1924, the Smith family moved south to Safety Harbor, and Goldie faithfully drank water from the mineral spring.

Today, that young girl, now known as Goldie Banks, is ninety-seven years old and has probably lived in Safety Harbor longer than any other current resident. The Espiritu Santo Springs may not be the mythical Fountain of Youth, but who can say that drinking the spring water regularly as a child didn't contribute to her long life span?

Chapter 9

THE DEVELOPMENT OF THE
COMMUNITY OF GREEN SPRINGS,
1885–1917

The early settlers were honest people. Their word was their bond. When a man said he would sell another a certain cow in his herd, we would have confidence that that man would not try to sneak out a few more, just because the owner would trust him to get the cow.
In everything the old friends knew and understood each other. When sickness or death came each neighbor allotted himself a task to help at this time.
—Gladys Ganley

As more and more settlers continued to arrive to the upper Pinellas peninsula, the beginnings of a community began to form. Although the log schoolhouse constructed by James McMullen and other pioneers in the mid-1850s had served as a makeshift church, the time had come for something more formal. So in 1886, the regional settlers organized the Sylvan Abbey Methodist Church, utilizing the name of the log cabin school. The church was located approximately midway between James McMullen's home and the community of Green Springs. Services continued there for nearly twenty years, into the early part of the twentieth century.

Around 1888, Captain George Washington and his son, C.S. Washington, erected a commercial dock in Green Springs, which was used to bring in supplies and ship out citrus. This dock was located about a mile north of the current city marina, just above Grand Central Avenue.

In 1890, near the location of the commercial dock, the first post office was established on Grand Central Avenue. By now, the town had become known as Green Springs, although this name was rejected for the post office due to potential confusion with the delivery of mail to the town of Green Cove Springs, located in the northeast portion of the state near Jacksonville. Instead, the post office was assigned the name Safety Harbor, in recognition of the small inlet adjacent to the settlement in the northwest portion of Old Tampa Bay. Sid Youngblood served as the first postmaster out of the grocery store he operated north of what would become the city limits. Mail to rural addresses was delivered by horseback. Later, the store closed when the post office was moved south to Main Street. The dock was moved as well.

Although people continued to flock to the Pinellas peninsula, the settlement remained mostly isolated due to the lack of viable transportation links to other communities. A railroad line through the area was completed in 1888, but it bypassed Green Springs entirely in favor of Tarpon Springs, Dunedin, Clear Water and Largo. Not unexpectedly, the growth of the county followed the path of the railroad tracks. As one early source summarized, "The towns reached by [the railroad] immediately began to grow; and the others, Anclote, Safety Harbor, Bayview, Anona, Indian Rocks and Disston, for years remained stationary." As the end of the line, St. Petersburg benefited the most from the railroad. Soon that settlement would grow to become the largest city of the peninsula and the center of most of its industry.

This seclusion had its drawbacks. A story passed down from the 1880s relates that an older man named Mr. Enlow was found stashed in his fireplace, his lifeless body surrounded by firewood in an apparent attempt to burn it. The perpetrator was not found, but according to McMullen and Booth descendant Gladys Ganley, a few years later a gunman dying in Texas confessed to the crime, explaining that he had heard that Mr. Enlow had hidden money in his house. This event produced a local superstition, again according to Ganley. "For years people would avoid going by the place, some would say the place was haunted...for years everyone seemed afraid of the place. Finally someone bought the property and demolished the hoax. A rebuilt house with paint really changed the story."

Almost all the homesteaders raised their own cows, chickens and hogs, and the animals were allowed to graze wherever they pleased. By fall, the ground would be covered by acorns, which were good food for the pigs. At the first cold spell, hogs would be killed, and the settlers would feast on fresh pork, sausage and chitterlings. The meat was smoked over a hickory wood fire and would be enjoyed by the settlers until they were ready for a change of diet, when they would cast nets for mullet. Without the availability of ice

Young members of the Green Springs Band before the city's incorporation as Safety Harbor in 1917. *Photo courtesy of Safety Harbor Museum and Cultural Center.*

Several buildings in early Safety Harbor. The store on the left is possibly Youngblood's Meat Market, a building destroyed by the fire in 1917. The sign on the building on the right reads, "W.O.W. (Woodman of the World) Camp 498." *Photo courtesy of Heritage Village Archives and Library.*

or refrigeration, some of the bones and less desirable pieces of meat were packed in brine for longer preservation.

At the start of the twentieth century, the economy of the new town relied primarily on the citrus industry and small farming. Tourists visited the mineral springs to bathe in their restorative waters, typically arriving either by ferry from Tampa or via stagecoach from Clearwater.[7] Accommodations were scarce at first but gradually increased with the construction of the Green Springs Inn and the Hankins Hotel on the south side of Main Street.

As the town continued to grow, a store was opened by George B. Thomas, who came from Tampa to recover his health. Thomas later would serve as postmaster, a job he eventually handed over to his wife, Emma, and later to his son, George B. Thomas Jr. Soon thereafter, E.A. Boyd built a two-story house on what is now First Avenue North, with a general store on the first floor. A drugstore and another grocery store sprouted up at the corner of Second Avenue and Main Street. Also nearby were a barbershop, justice's office, photographer and real estate business. At some point, an open-air dance hall was erected. Later, in 1914, Ben Tucker opened the first hardware store, shipping in the merchandise from Tampa.

In 1905, sermons at the Sylvan Abbey Church were discontinued. Using furnishings from the original building, some members established a new church in Green Springs, while other parishioners attended services at a "Friendship" church elsewhere. The new Green Springs church was constructed at the northwest corner of Second Street and Fourth Avenue. It was initially known as the Green Springs Methodist Episcopal Church, South, but sometime between 1917 and 1939, the church altered its name to become the Safety Harbor Methodist Episcopal Church, South. Today, this church can be visited at Heritage Village in Largo.

The fate of the original Sylvan Abbey Church building is unclear. According to a typewritten sketch of the church's history, it was purchased by a member of the McMullen family to be used as his home. Other accounts claim that church members dismantled the building and sold the lumber.

The loss of the Sylvan Abbey Church meant that the area children needed a new school building to receive their education, and for that the community utilized a two-room building behind where the fire station stands today on Main Street. This would be the first school in the city limits, although it

7. Once known as "Clear Water Harbor," the city officially modified its name to "Clearwater Harbor" in 1896 and later shortened it further to simply "Clearwater" approximately ten years later.

The walking bridge across Alligator Creek, originally built as a shortcut for children to get to school. *Photo courtesy of Safety Harbor Museum and Cultural Center.*

Early Main Street on a busy day. *Photo courtesy of Heritage Village Archives and Library.*

is unclear whether a new building was constructed or whether an already-existing structure was converted for this use. The school encompassed grades one through eight, while older students were required to attend high school in Clearwater.

During the first decade of the new century, many new subdivisions were constructed throughout the city to attract more residents. According to a city building survey conducted in 1994, these developments included the Green Springs Subdivision; Espiritu Santo Springs Subdivision; South Seminole Park; Spring Haven Addition to Green Springs; Harry Kennedy's Subdivision, which was located in the north section of town; and Leech and Strain's Addition to Green Springs. The community remained segregated, however, and about the same time, the Brooklyn and Jackson Park communities were created for black families. West Green Springs, Seminole Park and Holmes Subdivision were established a few years later, in 1914.

Fire occasionally plagued the new community, most notably a blaze that destroyed the Bayshore Hotel in 1908, which is believed to have been built by Mr. and Mrs. James Leverette in 1880. The hotel was located on South Bayshore Boulevard, directly behind the building currently utilized by the Safety Harbor Museum and Cultural Center. Curiously, both the fire and the hotel's existence were almost entirely forgotten until artifacts and a building foundation were discovered in 1989 during an excavation by members of the Suncoast Archaeology Society.

Before Pinellas County seceded from Hillsborough on January 1, 1912, all official business had to be conducted in Tampa. The trip was an all-day affair. Motorized ferries across the bay left from the long Safety Harbor dock early in the morning and disembarked at Port Tampa. Gladys Ganley recalled that the docks in Tampa were often lined with freighters from foreign

Ferries transported passengers to and from Tampa from the Safety Harbor pier. *Photo courtesy of Heritage Village Archives and Library.*

ports. "[I]t was an interesting sight to watch the ships [*sic*] elevators working tirelessly loading cattle, phosphate, oranges and other commodities for sale." There was just enough time to conduct business or do some shopping before the return voyage was ready to leave in the late afternoon.

After a long period of isolation, the town's development was spurred by the establishment of transportation routes through the immediate region. By 1910, the use of automobiles had started to become a vital part of American life, and roads were rapidly constructed throughout the state. The first major road through the area was constructed in 1916, which left Clearwater near the Gulf Coast and circled around the top of the bay on its way to Tampa. Today, this road is known as State Road 590, which snakes through Safety Harbor along since-renamed local streets before connecting to Philippe Parkway and continuing north. About the same time, the first rail link connected Safety Harbor to Tampa. Visitors continued to use water transport as well, providing multiple means of entry to the city. A local brochure printed in 1915 boasted that, "in addition to the new railroad, we have a strong steamboat corporation in process of organization, which will operate a line of boats from Safety Harbor to Port Tampa & Tampa, giving a double daily schedule."

In 1915, a man named A.G. Waldron started the town's first newspaper. Called the *Tropical Breeze*, the paper lasted approximately one year before it was discontinued. Not content to see the community without a newspaper, the community's board of trade approached A.E. Shower and proposed that he take over publication. Shower had previously been in the newspaper business up north, and although he had vowed "to forever stay out of the business of getting the news," he relented under "the urging of friends and the smell of printers [*sic*] ink." He renamed the newspaper the *Safety Harbor Herald* and, with the assistance of his wife, Edith, began the task of reporting and printing for the town's few residents and businesses. The first edition ran in June 1916 and was just four pages long. The *Herald* not only survived but also flourished under the stewardship of the Shower family. Within a few years, the paper had expanded to between twelve and sixteen pages and was unfailingly distributed each Friday morning, even on Christmas Day.

In 1916, a new three-story schoolhouse made of red brick was built on Fifth Avenue North and provided education for grades one through nine, replacing the smaller building located near Main Street.

During World War I, thirty-eight Safety Harbor residents served, and two, Carl W. Lawton and Frank Smallwood, lost their lives, each from

Two members of the McMullen family. *From left to right*: "Uncle Birt" and "G. Ward." *Photo courtesy of Safety Harbor Museum and Cultural Center.*

pneumonia while stationed stateside. Lawton's funeral was reported to be the first military memorial service ever held in Pinellas County.

During the early years of the twentieth century, the young people of the community provided their own entertainment by putting on plays, having parties at their homes and holding "chicken pilleaus," often at Lover's Oak. For these, the young men would obtain a big pot, usually an iron washtub. While the chicken and rice cooked, the attendees would play games until the pilleau was ready to be served, in time for everyone to return home by midnight or shortly thereafter. Often, music would be played on guitars, banjos and other stringed instruments, sometimes by the McMullen boys from nearby Bay View, who were said to have been musically inclined. Recalled Gladys Ganley, "The young people enjoyed this rustic fellowship. The wonderful people who took the time to play with them did a great work that will live always."

One visitor described the community in 1915 as follows:

Safety Harbor has religious, social and educational advantages which will compare favorably with any community of its size in the country, having a splendid graded school and three churches...It has one first-class hotel and needs more. It has numerous boarding houses and cottages. It has a strong bank and various other business houses, all of which are thriving...Here is where you can enjoy your own home either in summer or in winter; then let it during the other season at a good figure, thereby making your investment profitable all the year 'round.

A year later, another writer described "a new 20-room brick hotel, an up-to-date bathing establishment, a live Board of Trade, a new High School, and all the natural scenery and beauty one could wish for."

In 1917, the settlement abandoned its earlier name of Green Springs and officially incorporated as the City of Safety Harbor. As had already been the case with the naming of the post office, this change was designed to prevent confusion between the city and another community in northeast Florida called Green Cove Springs. The new name took some time to catch on, however. In 1929, W.L. Straub reported that "[e]ven to this day many know the city better by the name Green Springs, or Green's Spring."

❧ PART III ❧
THE COMMUNITY OF
SAFETY HARBOR
FROM 1917 TO TODAY

Chapter 10

DEVASTATION AND GROWTH
OF A NEW CITY

1917 TO THE "LAND BOOM"

Only a few months after Safety Harbor was incorporated as a city, a fire started at the Green Springs Inn close to midnight on September 1, 1917, and soon raged in the first block of Main Street, both north and south, reducing all but one of the town's buildings to ash. As reported the following day by the *St. Petersburg Daily Times*, the fire "quickly wiped out of existence [the Green Springs Inn] and its contents." The fire likewise destroyed a boys' clothing store, a grocery store, a drugstore, a barbershop and Youngblood's meat market. It also "put out of commission every telephone in the village."

At the time, the small town had only recently held its first election. The previous month, on August 7, G.W. Campbell had been voted as Safety Harbor's first mayor, and J.S. Carivile and Dr. Byrd McMullen were elected as the first city commissioners. Safety Harbor did not have a fire department; in fact, just a few weeks earlier, citizens had rejected a proposal to purchase a chemical engine, therefore leaving the city ill prepared and unprotected from such a disaster.

After hearing the fire alarm—gunshot blasts—all who were able to help formed a bucket brigade while others did their best to save neighbors' belongings. The city called on nearby communities for help, but that night Clearwater's fire department, only six miles away, did not come. Clearwater's mayor refused to allow the pumping apparatus to help its neighboring town. Even though Clearwater's fire chief was unable to obtain a fire truck, he went to Safety

The aftermath of the 1917 fire that destroyed downtown Safety Harbor. *Photo courtesy of Heritage Village Archives and Library.*

Harbor anyway, to do what he could to help. It was the Tampa Fire Department that responded. Unfortunately, the causeway didn't yet exist, so Safety Harbor could be accessed only by traveling around the bay. After the long trip, they arrived just in time to assist the bucket brigade in saving the post office.

Bertha Rountree was the granddaughter of Mayor Campbell, and later, her brother Paul McElveen would become mayor as well. As children, Mrs. Rountree and her brother witnessed the fire from their parents' hotel, the St. Frances, one of the few buildings to survive. In 1992, she was quoted in *Remembering Safety Harbor* as saying, "My dad was sick at the time, but he told my brother to hitch up the team of mules and help people haul out their things. We stood on the front porch of our hotel and could see the flames leaping. The block across from the Spa burnt, but only that one block."

Almost one hundred years after that fire, residents still question why the neighboring fire department did not come to the rescue of "the little town on the bay." The *St. Petersburg Daily Times* posited that "under the influence of a northwest wind, the flames would probably soon burn themselves out." The *Daily Times* further reported that the St. Petersburg department was prepared to assist and had received approval from Mayor Lang, but it was decided that "the fire would have done its worst" long before the trip would be completed.

The Green Springs Inn, before it was destroyed by the 1917 fire. *Photo courtesy of Heritage Village Archives and Library.*

Although the city would recover from this tragedy, fire continued to threaten the community. A year later the home of Mr. and Mrs. B.R. Tucker was destroyed by a "Demon Fire," which the *Safety Harbor Herald* referenced as having "once again" visited the community. Because Safety Harbor homes were made of wood, fire was not uncommon, but when someone needed help, neighbors pulled together. Life went on.

Disease threatened countywide when two outbreaks of the Spanish flu hit in 1918 and again the following March. As residents had no organized garbage collection, much of the garbage was piled in specific locations throughout town, out in the open. During the outbreaks, residents were urged to be careful with slops and were asked to burn refuse and use lime, which was given out at the newspaper's office.

By now, Safety Harbor boasted a population of around two hundred individuals. White business owners and those in government lived closest to Main Street. Visitors coming for the "healing waters" often camped near the mineral springs. Across town, in the areas that are now near Elm and Pine Streets, black neighbors lived in what was referred to as the "Quarters." Weeds and brush grew tall along roadsides, and cedar sidewalks lined the brick-paved Main Street. Family gardens took up plots the size of current lots. There were few homes scattered throughout town, but the residents of the newly incorporated city looked for ways to improve it.

Safety Harbor's tax base of $416,045 was limited in 1918, but the town council began to fund projects to improve infrastructure, including the establishment of water, gas and sewer service. Although only an estimated fifty houses were wired for electricity, more would soon follow.

Not long after the new decade began, the city borrowed $1 million through the issuance of bonds to fund development projects. Granite sidewalks were installed "from the springs to the depot." But the city government didn't stop there. Residents voted on bond issues to build better schools. Dredge and fill operations were approved to construct a dock. Between the seawall and the bay, twenty acres of marshy land were filled for the construction of future homes, which instead became the site of the Safety Harbor Resort and Spa.

The community grew. A pier was constructed on the urging of citizens and Shower's editorials in the *Herald* and the dock was completed. A new, larger pool was built at Espiritu Santo Springs. The city also focused on creating a road "along the bay shore." Articles on the progress of these projects and others filled the front page of the newspaper. But these efforts would mostly be for naught.

In 1921, only a few residents would have remembered the hurricane of 1848, but they experienced devastation firsthand when a major hurricane hit the Pinellas peninsula that year. The storm water surged through the bay and washed away roads, trees and homes. The fish house at the end of the dock, where fisherman dried their nets and relaxed after unloading their catch, was destroyed. The dance hall that had been constructed at the end of the pier floated inland and cut into buildings along the shore. Perhaps the worst hit, according to the October 28, 1921 edition of the *Safety Harbor Herald*, was the Espiritu Santo Springs Corporation and all of its recent improvements, including the pool, bottling house, dance hall, docks and bathhouses. Ward McMullen, born in 1870, and the son of James P. "Captain Jim" McMullen, recalled the hurricane of 1921 in an undated recorded interview sometime before his death in 1965. He described the winds and the resulting damage and added, "It was pretty bad. It blowed down five oak trees around my house."

After the second disaster to impact the city in four years, the townspeople took charge. The Espiritu Santo Springs Corporation built the Pipkin and Pavilion buildings at the sanatorium to replace the wooden structures that

The St. James Hotel. *Photo courtesy of Safety Harbor Museum and Cultural Center.*

had been destroyed by the hurricane. At the same time, Virginia Tucker built a grand Colonial Revival mansion, which still stands just north of the Safety Harbor Resort and Spa. She also began construction on the St. James Hotel, named for her husband, James Felix Tucker, who died in 1913. The St. James was originally intended to house guests visiting the sanatorium but also contained a grocery store, a restaurant and a drugstore, as well as a terminal for the Florida Motor Lines. The modern hotel, which opened on March 6, 1925, had a phone in every room, hot and cold running water, private baths and electric lights. At that time, these were uncommon amenities for a hotel in a small city.

In 1923, further developments were platted throughout the city, including Lincoln Heights, South Green Springs Replat and, in 1924, Safety Harbor Heights. The year 1925 brought De Soto Estates, Dixie Subdivision, Harbor Highlands, Harbor Hill Park, Mira-Mar Terrace and Washington-Brennan. Other development was happening as well. On September 6, 1924, a bridge connecting Safety Harbor and Oldsmar opened, which helped those coming to Safety Harbor or those traveling to Tampa. It was the first bridge across Old Tampa Bay for use by automobiles.

George F. Washburn bought properties along First Avenue and Main Street, currently the location of the city's public library, where he built the Alden apartment building. The Alden also was home to the city's first movie theater and, even twenty years later, would be a place where a movie could be

Looking south from (the currently named) Philippe Parkway: The Alden Apartments, St. James Hotel and the Silver Dome Apartments. *Photo courtesy of Heritage Village Archives and Library.*

seen for less than a dime. Washburn also built the Silver Dome Apartments, nicknamed for its distinctive metallic domes. For business owners and residents alike, the future looked promising. The year was 1925, in the midst of Florida's land boom, and the town had doubled to a population of five hundred. Property values were skyrocketing. According to St. Petersburg cattleman Jay Starkey:

> *In Pinellas County some properties changed ownership several times within one year. I remember buying a five-acre tract one morning and selling it that afternoon at a $500 profit. That was chicken feed, compared to many deals that I heard about. The thing that is hard to understand if you were not here, was that vacant lots and acreage were bought for one purpose in 95 percent of the sales. That was to re-sell. Men and some women of every walk of life, bought real estate salesman licenses and got into the act, sometimes selling to one another. Everybody made money for a while.*

The city of Safety Harbor seemed better suited than most communities to take advantage of this frenzy that gripped investors during the early 1920s.

According to the Historic Building Survey completed by Historic Property Associates, Incorporated, in 1994:

> *It offered an attractive setting, laid out on the shores of Old Tampa Bay by the well-known mineral springs and near the continually expanding urban center of St. Petersburg and the Gulf beaches. There was a large amount of open land available for development, which ultimately proved an irresistible attraction for the hordes of speculators who descended upon the state during the period that became known as the "Great Florida Land Boom."*

The city took out more bonds for improvements, borrowing money that would later be impossible to pay back. No one seemed to notice that the city's financial health was supported by a house of cards.

BUSTED

City leaders believed Safety Harbor would flourish, but instead the city's debt grew as the land boom came to an end. Banks crashed, and like the rest of the country, Florida fell into deeper financial trouble. New development was halted. Many lost their land and homes to foreclosure, and those who had come during the boom years moved away. Homes once occupied were left vacant, as were many of the businesses on Main Street. Most of the city's remaining population depended on federal relief programs. The city's water supply was bad, and $12,000 was needed to repair and maintain city services. Buildings and infrastructure were in desperate need of repair. Even the once-popular springs seemed to have a hopeless future.

New Deal programs brought federal assistance. New homes were built when agencies such as the Federal Housing Authority allowed prospective homeowners to obtain financing for new construction. The Works Progress Administration is mentioned frequently in the *Safety Harbor Herald*, not only because it provided work, but also because its funding contributed to expansion of local infrastructure, such as for a library and adjacent park.

In 1935, the Davis Causeway was completed across Tampa Bay. The project provided jobs, but since it bypassed Safety Harbor for Clearwater, it led to fewer people passing through. Many residents, led by Mayor Louis Zinsser, opposed construction of the causeway on environmental grounds, believing that the heavy construction would obstruct flushing of the bay.

People came from near and far for Espritu Santo Springs water. *Photo courtesy of Heritage Village Archives and Library.*

Zinsser and other city leaders likely foresaw that rerouting traffic away from Safety Harbor would negatively affect the city's economy, which proved true.

By now, the city's municipal debt was approximately $1,070,000, represented by bonds that had a combined value of $763,000, and $300,000 in defaulted interest. Seeking relief, the city proposed a refinancing plan, which was approved by all bondholders, including the Bank of Dunedin:

> *My father, the president of this bank, as well as this writer, have been familiar with the financial difficulties of our neighboring town of Safety Harbor, which has for some years been regarded as the worst financial situation in Florida...*
> *[W]e have carefully gone over the refunding plans which are now being signed up by the bondholders with the City, and we believe that this plan is all that the property owners can function under, and that it is the only possible plan which is fair and just to all parties concerned.*

Insurance claims were an easy answer for a few property owners, and several homes in the city burned down under suspicious circumstances. In August 1937, the *Herald* reported on one such instance: "[A] car was seen to stop across the street from the house. A short time after the car drove away and in a few minutes flames were seen to shoot from the building. The fire did not last long but while it was going it was plenty hot."

That same year, under the new Wilcox Municipal Bankruptcy Act, the city was reportedly the first municipality in the country to declare bankruptcy. Through restructuring, Safety Harbor's debt went from over $1 million to $375,000, which still would take thirty-three years to pay off.

Population dramatically changed after the boom. In 1930, there were 765 people living in Safety Harbor; by 1935, there were only 583. Part of this decrease was due to paring back the city limits by five hundred acres in an effort to reduce the cost of services provided to residents. But by 1940, the city's population had risen again to 694.

Although the city was small and in financial disarray, there were still many visitors to the springs, and in 1936, a letter to the *Herald*'s editor called for a community address book to be kept at the post office:

> *The city is very small but the population seems to be a floating one and it seems to be impossible to keep pace with it. People come and go and some are known only to a very few. Again folks come and live with relatives by a different name than that which they bear, so it is very hard to locate them. On New Year's Day the man who delivers telegrams hunted from door to door for a lady for whom he had a telegram and no one seemed to have ever heard the name.*

It is no surprise that a telegram was difficult to deliver; even into the 1940s, street addresses were not used by city residents. Businesses advertised as being located "close to the springs" or "on Main Street," leaving it up to potential customers to find their way. One envelope at the Safety Harbor Museum and Cultural Center's postal display is a perfect example of those times. The envelope is postmarked Miami, Florida, December 19, 1936, and is addressed simply to Susan H. Tucker, Espiritu Santo Springs, Florida.

EVERYDAY LIFE IN THE HARBOR TO THE 1930S

Since pioneer days, livestock were free to roam the city at will. In the first few decades after the city's incorporation, cows could be staked anywhere there was grass, as long as someone remembered to water them. Children

Safety Harbor's early Main Street shops sold cigars, groceries, furniture and more. *Photo courtesy of Heritage Village Archives and Library.*

often went barefoot, and families relied on fruit trees and vegetable gardens. People hunted wild game throughout Safety Harbor's vast undeveloped areas and caught plenty of fish in the bay. Most streets were sand until the early 1920s, and other than the few years of the land boom, there was little funding to handle the costs of sewer and water services, let alone major improvements to roads or sidewalks. Limited funds meant that the elected officials debated the best way to spend what little money the city had.

Entertainment often revolved around the churches: Methodist, Presbyterian, Baptist, Nazarene and Episcopal. The community gathered for meetings of the Women's Civic Club, Kiwanis, Eastern Star, the Masons, Royal Neighbors, Modern Woodmen of America and Woodmen of the World. Both men and women passed the time by playing shuffleboard, tennis and croquet.

There were also summer baseball games to attend. From the late teens to the 1930s, the newspaper encouraged residents to "Cheer on the Safety Harbor Boys." The team of young men was referred to for a short time as the "Sluggers" and at other times as the "Safety Harbor Diamond Ball Team" but appeared to never have been given a formal name. The players changed with each new season. The team made the weekly paper and was sometimes its only sports news. Safety Harbor was called to support the "Boys" with financial help as well as encouragement. Games were played on a field located in today's current waterfront park, behind the spa, against Tarpon Springs, Oldsmar, St. Petersburg, Clearwater and other neighboring communities. During some years, there was also a girls' softball team that played in the school's baseball diamond, and many came out to cheer them on as well. For a time, too, boxing exhibitions attracted many to an evening match in a temporary outdoor ring.

Fish fries brought the town together to feast on fish, sweet potatoes, fresh vegetables, home-baked pies and sweets. These events were often organized to raise money for the local churches. The Lover's Oak tree was another hangout, especially for children and teenagers. In a memoir written during a visit to Safety Harbor in 1929, Elizabeth Snedecor Campbell, whose family built a log cabin in 1876 (which is still located on Sixth Street South), wrote:

> *This afternoon I have been to the old oak tree—The Picnic Tree—we all used to call it, where George and I played when we were little children. I could pick out the branch on which we had a swing, and the ones where we had nailed some boards and had a "tree house." The blue water of the bay looked as blue and beautiful now as it did then.*

Residents took advantage of the occasional opportunity to leave town once or twice a year to go to Tampa or another nearby city. One favorite attraction was the annual circus show. In an early account, the *Herald* reported, "Monday was circus day in Tampa and despite the rainy day the greater part of Safety Harbor was there. According to very reliable reports over 1500 autos passed through town on the way to the big Ringling Bros. show—and it was some show too."

The town was still getting accustomed to automobile traffic, and unfortunately, there was a high number of accidents, especially on Main Street, where residents were still used to going wherever they pleased. In 1929, the changing technology and faster pace ensnared "Keeter" Booth, who seventy-five years earlier had been the first child of European descent born on the Pinellas peninsula:

> *What might have been a most serious accident took place on Main [S]treet last Friday night when "Uncle Keeter" Booth was going to the boxing exhibition held in the Pitkin Park. Mr. Booth was riding his horse as usual when a Ford car driven by Ben Downs, accompanied by his father, ran into him. Mr. Booth was thrown from his horse, and land[ed] on top of the car, according to the information at hand, and skinned one of his legs pretty*

badly. However he was not hurt seriously and after the dazed spell worked off, got on his horse and rode to town. It is supposed that young Downs was partially blinded by passing autos either with one light or with brights on. The Ford was damaged quite a bit in the accident. Court was held on Saturday morning and the order issued as a result of the accident that in the future the ordinance against boys under 16 driving cars will be enforced.

Others weren't as lucky. On October 10, 1931, five-year-old Clyde Rigsby and his twin brother, Claude, had just left a birthday party with several friends, including their three-year-old cousin, Earl Denton. The *Herald* reported, "Happy as little children are, and not thinking of any possible harm, little Earl tore away from the other children...The child was hit by the slowly moving car and thrown to the brick pavement." The elderly driver, it was said, fainted when she realized what she had done.

"Earl's sister screamed," Clyde Rigsby, now eighty-eight, recently recalled. "My dad was coming from Clearwater in an old Model-A Ford and he could hear her at the railroad tracks...I can see him to this day."

Earl Denton died almost immediately. At the funeral the following day, the church was "packed to capacity and many could not gain entrance."

A few years later, an artist was hired to paint stop signs along Main Street. Warnings were issued to drivers to obey the traffic rules, but still, accidents continued.

Chapter 11

THE HISTORY AND DEVELOPMENT
OF THE SAFETY HARBOR SPA

Safety Harbor's best economic resource proved to be its water. Tourists continued to flock to the city to enjoy the restorative powers of the natural mineral springs. The Espiritu Santo Springs Corporation (the successor to James and Virginia Tucker's interests) eyed development, hoping to become the next Saratoga Springs. In the mid-1920s, it constructed and began operating the St. James Hotel, which was located across the street from the primary facility and was intended to provide additional rooms to guests. At this time, too, the Espiritu Santo Springs Corporation began selling subdivision properties, believing that a vast economy would be built around the springs.

By then, the spring water was being bottled and sold nationally. W.E. Sinclair, the corporation's vice-president and general manager, boasted that "the Springs are a gold mine: Shipments of water are made of [*sic*] all parts of the United States: and the only expenses are the cost of bottles and the expense of bottling...[W]ith the Sanitarium developed and the Turkish Baths and the Swimming Pool, together with our large Hotel, I consider we will have one of the biggest and best paying investments in the State of Florida."

All of this activity brought not only a diverse clientele to the small town but also other developers and entrepreneurs interested in taking advantage of the claimed medicinal-like qualities of the water. One such person was Dr. Con F. Barth, who, in the summer of 1928, opened Dr. Barth's Hotel & Baths, another hotel and mineral health establishment, utilizing the waters

Label for a half gallon of water from one of the four mineral springs. *Courtesy of Safety Harbor Museum and Cultural Center.*

drawn from the nearby Pipkin Mineral Wells. Dr. Barth was a successful boxing trainer, having worked with at least one middleweight champion, Albert "Buck" Crouse. Dr. Barth would later involve himself in the social and political life of the city, serving as a city commissioner in the mid-1930s and as mayor from 1950 to 1952.

In the fall of 1929, the Pipkin Mineral Wells Hotel was sold to C.L. Nisely of Springfield, Ohio, and was renamed the Spa Park Inn. By December, Nisely's establishment had been remodeled and the grounds beautified with shrubbery. The Pipkin springs, which had previously flowed through an old pump house, were transferred to a "beautiful outdoor fountain where they [could] be had by any one." Barth's institute adjoining Spa Park Inn was included in the extensive improvement program, providing it with larger quarters and greater facilities.

By the end of the 1920s, Safety Harbor boasted three hotels specifically catering to health through the use of the water from different springs. People came by train, boat and car, some just for the water and others to relax and recover from a bout of poor health. Around this time, the Tuckers' former facility at Espiritu Santo Springs became known as the General Sanitarium, Inc. Business was booming. Then, seemingly overnight, everything fell apart. The "Florida Land Boom" was over, and the Great Depression had begun.

Postcard depicting Dr. Barth's Hotel & Baths. *Photo courtesy of Safety Harbor Museum and Cultural Center.*

By the mid-1930s, many of the homes and businesses in the small city had been abandoned. The economy built around the mineral springs was not spared. The fifty-eight-room St. James Hotel closed and was stripped of all fixtures and furnishings. For the next several years the buildings were vacant and began deteriorating. Eventually, the facilities so lovingly built by the Baileys and the Tuckers fell into the hands of the State of Florida.

In 1936, Dr. Alben Jansik, an Austrian physician from Palm Beach, purchased the springs, sanitarium and the St. James Hotel at a tax sale for approximately $17,000. Dr. Jansik, who had come from the Garment District of New York, renovated and redecorated the existing structures, improved the landscaping and created recreation facilities such as shuffleboard and lawn tennis courts. A forty-five- by ninety-five-foot swimming pool was built through which eight thousand gallons of spring water flowed daily. The *St. Petersburg Times* reported that there was a 280-acre farm nearby from which fresh vegetables would be available for the tables in the dining room.

Dr. Jansik's efforts proved successful. Soon, tourist literature described the resort as "a Florida haven for those in search of health, recreation and rest." Wealthy families and celebrities flocked to the facility, reportedly including the widow of illusionist Harry Houdini, department store founders F.W. Grant and Russ Kresge and the Seagram family from Canada, who created what would become the largest distiller of alcoholic beverages in the world. Also, a dozen professional golfers and their wives visited prior to their participation in a tournament in nearby Belleair in 1937, including Gene Sarazen, then one of the world's top-ranked players. During one memorable week of spring training in 1940, the entire Brooklyn Dodgers team stayed at the St. James Hotel, perhaps on the recommendation of the widow of Charles H. Ebbets, former owner of the Dodgers, who was an occasional guest herself.

When World War II broke out in 1939, however, business suffered, and by the early 1940s, the facility was being operated primarily as a rehabilitation facility for recovering alcoholics. According to an unpublished but authorized history of the spa drafted in 1966, "The lack of adequate income accompanied by mounting necessary repairs forced the proprietors to place the Espiritu Santo Springs property on the market in 1945." Later that year, the property was purchased by Dr. Salem Baranoff, whom Dr. Jansik had previously brought in to assist him in the winter months, and the facility entered its next phase.

Dr. Salem Baranoff

Like the pioneers and early settlers, Salem Baranoff was not native to the region but soon after his arrival became a prominent member of the Safety Harbor community. Born in Kiev, he immigrated to New York City with his family as a teenager in 1904. There, while teaching in a Hebrew school and studying English, he developed an interest in healing through natural processes. Although other members of his family had become rabbis, he wanted to be a doctor instead. "I was a bit of a rebel," he told a reporter a few years before his death.

After graduating from the American School of Naturopathy in 1921, Dr. Baranoff became a practitioner of this form of alternative medicine that spurns surgery and drugs in favor of natural health methods. From his office in Brownsville, a predominantly Jewish neighborhood in eastern Brooklyn, New York, Dr. Baranoff focused on the benefits of proper diet and physical fitness, learning to minimize the effects of the aging process so that people could age gracefully. His regimen for healthful living through diet and exercise proved so successful that one of his patients soon offered him his summer house near Spring Valley to use for the development of a health resort.

Dr. Baranoff's Health Resort in Safety Harbor. *Photo courtesy of Heritage Village Archives and Library.*

When that property proved unsuitable for Dr. Baranoff's plans, he rented an old closed hotel for clients in Spring Valley instead and began to promote an ideology of natural health. He operated this health resort for nineteen years. During this time, he continued to maintain offices in New York City and had a weekly radio program in Yiddish to discuss nature, diet and health, believed to have been one of the earliest radio shows focusing on health foods. Because his facility in Spring Valley was available for only a limited period of time each year, he decided to spend his winters assisting Dr. Jansik at the Safety Harbor Sanitarium.

In 1945, Dr. Baranoff purchased the entire eighteen-acre complex, including several buildings and the five mineral springs, for $190,000. He intended to pattern the facility after the town of Spa in Belgium and similar mineral waters in Austria and Germany, where people would come to bathe in the mineral springs and to drink the water to restore their health, to create a true resort health spa with on-site accommodations to house overnight visitors. The modern Safety Harbor Spa was born.

Dr. Baranoff Leads the Spa Forward

During the first season under Dr. Baranoff's control, 150 people traveled from New York to stay at the spa. Some were former Baranoff clients from his Spring Valley facility, but others were drawn by advertisements placed in the *New York Times* or by word of mouth. Management of the facility was a family affair: Salem's wife, Lisa, served as the dietician, and her sister, Dena, was the physical therapist. Upon arrival, guests would receive a physical examination and be assigned individualized diets, as well as a variety of exercises, massages and whirlpool baths. Once again, the former St. James Hotel was used for guests and renamed the De Soto Hotel. Spa workers crossed the street between buildings when their jobs required it. There was plenty of entertainment, too, organized by a recreation director. All in all, Dr. Baranoff designed a complete program to improve his guests' physical and mental health.

In many respects, Dr. Baranoff's philosophy of health and life was ahead of its time. He advocated a holistic program that incorporated a proper diet, proper thoughts, proper exercise and adequate rest. He developed a list of "ten commandments" for his clients to follow in order to have a happier, healthier and longer life. These were:

> Thou shall respect thy body as the highest manifestation of life.
> Thou shall abstain from all unnatural devitalized food and stimulating beverages.
> Thou shall nourish thy body with only natural unprocessed live food that thou shall extend thy years in health for loving, charitable service.
> Thou shall regenerate thy body by the right balance of activity and rest.
> Thou shall purify thy cells, tissue, and blood with pure fresh air and sunshine.
> Thou shall abstain from all foods when out of sorts in mind and body.
> Thou shall keep thy thoughts, words, and emotions, pure, calm, and uplifting.
> Thou shall increase thy knowledge of nature's laws, abide therewith and enjoy the fruits of thy life's labor.
> Thou shall lift up thyself and thy brother with thine own obedience to all nature's laws.
> Thou shall stretch thy 600 muscles daily, maintain a positive attitude at all times, and count thy blessings regularly.

Postcard of Safety Harbor Sanatorium and Espiritu Santo Springs. *Photo courtesy of Safety Harbor Museum and Cultural Center.*

"I've seen people who follow this program at Safety Harbor Spa and they have benefited by it," Dr. Baranoff was quoted as saying. "I've seen people who come in wheelchairs and, in a couple months, they were on their own and lived another thirty-forty years, living the proper life...Learn how to live. Live and learn how to live...Incidentally, this is also preventive medicine."

The spa gained immense popularity under Dr. Baranoff's stewardship. He extolled the benefits of naturopathic medicine, combined with the therapeutic properties of the mineral water. In the early 1950s, he partnered with two other physicians, including Dr. Richard Gubner, who soon took a controlling interest. Their goal was to turn the resort into a modern-day wellness retreat, offering massages, mineral and steam baths, health foods and hot packs. People from all over the world arrived seeking not only the curative powers of the waters but also to relax and to immerse themselves in a healthy regimen that included diet and exercise. Some stayed for the entire season.

Many New Yorkers and other northerners came down for the waters and health programs, including celebrities such as famed attorney Louis Nizer and frequent guest Kivie Kaplan, the national chairman of the NAACP. In addition, professional athletes used the property as a training facility while they searched for therapeutic remedies from the springs.

The spa employed primarily Safety Harbor, Clearwater and Oldsmar residents. According to longtime resident David Nichols, "There were plenty of people standing in line for your job; everybody wanted to work for them."

For local workers, that meant an intense schedule that began the first of September and lasted every day until the middle of April, with no days off.

The spa's wealthy guests tipped well, and spa jobs were considered good opportunities for people who wanted to work close to home. According to former resident Sandie Brasfield, "Everybody who lived in Safety Harbor worked at the spa at some point." Dolly Brader Whitehead, another former Safety Harbor resident, recalled her time spent as a juice girl in 1956 and 1957:

> *I worked in the De Soto Hotel. It belonged to the spa. I had to squeeze the orange juice and grapefruit juice. There was a big room in the basement of the spa where the wells were. The wells were numbered one, two, three and four. We'd come in the morning at five o'clock for the juicer, and we'd set up. Then we'd take our trays of prune juice, grapefruit juice and orange juice. The hotel had three stories, and I used an elevator that you had to run yourself. I had to get it level with the floor, and I had trays of juice to carry. I would knock on doors and deliver the glasses, then pick up the glasses, take them back and wash them and then go home. And then we'd come back at two o'clock in the afternoon.*

About her task of preparing afternoon snacks for guests, Mrs. Whitehead added:

> *We had to section grapefruit—we probably sectioned six bushels of grapefruit—and we put them in bowls and lined them up on the counter. People would pour honey and gelatin all over them. Then we'd have to wash the bowls, then go home, and then we'd come back at eight o'clock and serve tea to all the guests who played cards in the basement.*

Like Mrs. Whitehead, David Nichols also prepared grapefruit at the spa, and he soon became quite popular with some of the clients, who would spend hours in the basement drinking tea, eating grapefruit and playing gin and other card games after their evening exercise. "While the guests were taking their walks, I was cutting grapefruit," Nichols recently said. "I'd bring a salt shaker from home and I'd cut them in half, put salt on them, and put honey in the hole." For these guests, forced to endure strict salt-free diets, Nichols's preparation technique proved irresistible, and they lavished him with generous tips. "I was making more money than carpenters and electricians," he recalled. When Dr. Baranoff discovered what was going on, he declined to address the dietary violation directly with his resourceful employee but merely remarked on "how a young man had discovered a method of making money using a commodity as inexpensive as salt," while admitting that he had already seen some of his guests sneaking into local restaurants to eat French fries, hamburgers and other fare.

In 1963, only two years after being hired as a yoga instructor by Dr. Gubner, Salu Devnani became general manager of the Safety Harbor Spa. Born in Pakistan, Mr. Devnani moved with his mother and five siblings to Bombay. He later moved to Jamaica and, finally, the United States. He worked hard to earn a college degree and gave credit to his ethics and beliefs for his business success.

Mr. Devnani was an outspoken Safety Harbor businessman and leader, driven by a strong set of ideals. His wife, Mrs. Susanne Devnani, remembered their time at the spa: "Everybody loved my husband. He was a very outgoing person." She also recalled the spa's wealthy clientele, including lawyers, doctors and entertainers, as well as members of the mafia. She added that during the 1960s and 1970s, "We were closed in the summertime. There was nothing— you could look to the street and not see one car." But when the spa's patrons returned, Safety Harbor thrived. "We used to give the water away. One had more magnesium," she said. "One smelled a little—it had sulfur. People really did come for their health."

With Mr. Devnani's help, the spa continued to grow. By 1966, the facility had added two new buildings, the Bay Pavilion and the Spring Pavilion, which offered "individually controlled thermostats, the latest model RCA televisions [*sic*] sets with remote control, and soft, plush carpeting and furnishings of olive teakwood in modern Spanish design." Many of the newer rooms had "either balconies or terraces providing guests with picturesque views of the blue waters of the Bay."

Recreation options expanded as well. A driving range was constructed, supported by the resort's own PGA pro. A carpeted gymnasium housed the latest in gym equipment and offered popular exercise classes taught by a qualified instructor. An art and ceramics studio and dance studio were added. After-dinner activities included a different form of entertainment each evening, such as movies, professional performers and health lectures, often in the auditorium located in the Spring Pavilion.

A variety of treatments were offered, too. The resident physician would schedule daily massages, swimming in the mineral water, steam and sauna baths, solariums and rest. Electrotherapy and physiotherapy were administered by a medical team, which included a medical director, a licensed physician, a chiropractor and bathhouse assistants.

By 1973, there were approximately two hundred staff members and four hundred guests at the facility. Annual profits, which were $500,000 in 1961, increased to over $6 million by 1981.

The Spa Today

After Dr. Baranoff's death at the age of ninety in July 1977, the spa continued to flourish. During the 1980s and early 1990s, for example, many top-ranked professional boxers came to the resort for training, preferring the tranquil setting and health benefits of the spa to working out in big-city gyms. These included former champions and all-time greats Sugar Ray Leonard and Evander Holyfield, former light middleweight champion John "The Beast" Mugabi, former welterweight champion Mark Breland, title contender Tony Sibson, British heavyweight champion Gary Mason, John Mundunga, Alex Stewart and Francisco Arreola, who now trains boxers in nearby Tampa.

Gradually, however, due to changing tastes and increased competition from other resorts, the spa experienced a declining customer base. As described on the spa's own website, "People from around the world were coming to Florida for other reasons, enticed by numerous new Florida attractions built nearby in Central Florida, beautiful white beaches and lifestyle trends that were not conducive to creating a consciousness and demand for healthy living choices."

In 2004, the spa was purchased by the Olympia Development Group, Inc., of Dunedin, Florida for $25 million and underwent a multimillion-dollar renovation. By 2008, however, the real estate market had collapsed, and revenues from the resort decreased dramatically. In October 2010, the resort filed to reorganize under Chapter 11 bankruptcy protection, emerging nine months later after a federal judge approved its proposed financial restructuring plan. Around the same time, the spa agreed to sell thirteen acres of waterfront property to the city, which has since been converted into a public park.

Adding to the city's lore are reports that the spa might be haunted. The ghost of Dr. Baranoff is said to move salt and pepper shakers, doors have been mysteriously opened throughout the facility and voices have been heard in empty parts of the building. In the 1990s, telephone calls from empty rooms in the midst of renovations were allegedly placed to the front desk.

In 1964, the Safety Harbor Spa was designated a historical landmark by the U.S. Department of the Interior, and in 1997 it became a Florida Heritage Landmark. Today, the facility continues to operate, offering a spa and fitness center to vacationers and local residents and providing thirty thousand square feet of space for wedding receptions and conferences. Mineral water drawn from three of the springs is available to guests at the Fountain Grille Restaurant and from coolers located throughout the facility.

Chapter 12

THE RAILROAD

The mid-nineteenth century witnessed a boom in railway construction throughout the United States. By 1860, the railroad had mostly replaced water transport over rivers and canals as the primary means of travel. A few years later, in 1869, the first transcontinental railway link was completed at Promontory Summit in Utah. Soon, nearly the entire country was connected to the network of rails.

Yet the region's early settlers remained isolated. As briefly mentioned in Chapter 9, the first railroad through the Pinellas peninsula wasn't completed until 1888. The brainchild of a Russian immigrant named Peter Demens, the Orange Belt Railway connected St. Petersburg to either Lacoochee or Sanford to the northeast, where travelers could transfer to other lines. But the tracks ran through the central and western parts of the peninsula, completely bypassing Green Springs and other nearby settlements such as Bay View in favor of Tarpon Springs, Dunedin and Clear Water. The nearest station for local residents was in Largo, and it was to this depot that they would cart their citrus for shipment.

Within a year of completing his railroad, however, Demens was forced to sell the line due to financial difficulties. Soon, the Orange Belt entered receivership and was reorganized as the Sanford and St. Petersburg Railway. In 1895, the system was leased to Henry Plant, who offered connecting service through his own train lines all the way to Jacksonville. Despite these changes, the nearest point of access to the railroad for local residents remained Largo. As a result, the growth of Green Springs slowed, while settlements better serviced by the train flourished.

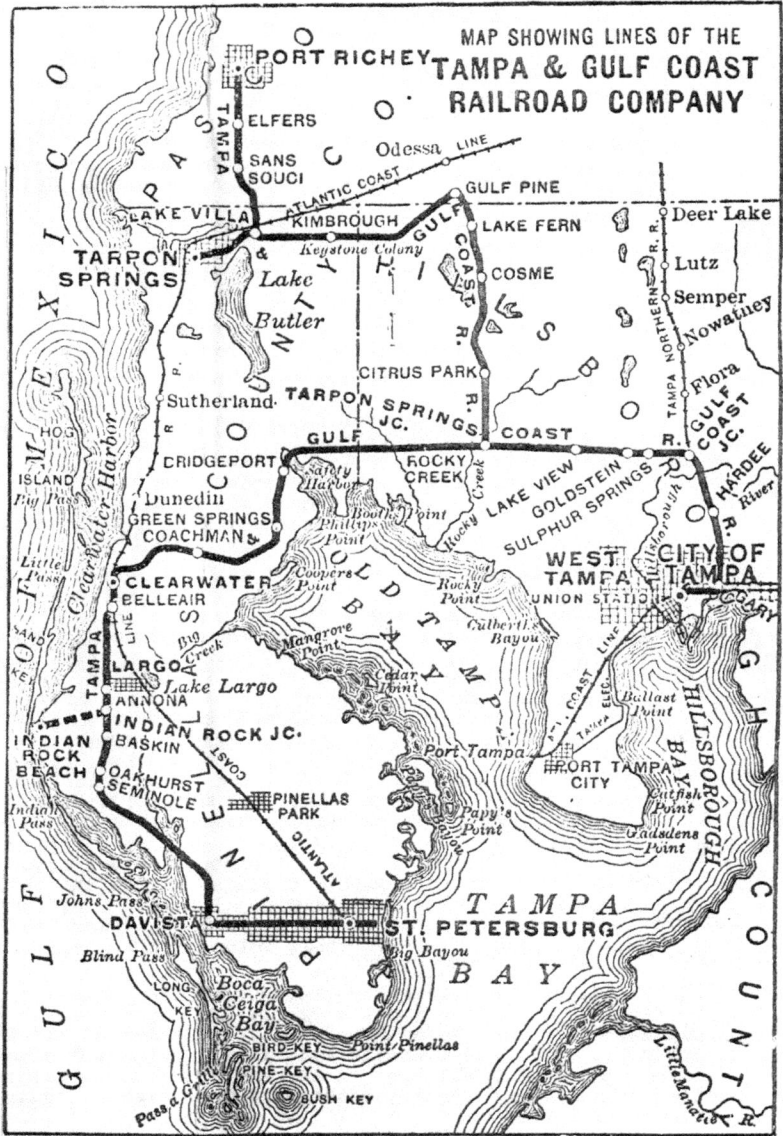

Map of the routes served by the Tampa & Gulf Coast Railroad Company throughout the Tampa Bay region. *Courtesy of Tom Pavluvcik.*

The situation would continue for another fifteen long years. Finally, in 1909, the wheels of change were set into motion when a group of Hillsborough businessmen led by a sawmill owner and builder named Charles Lutz purchased a rail route owned and operated by the Gulf Pine logging company. The route was short, running only from the current-day community of Lutz to a sawmill located approximately eleven miles east of Tarpon Springs. But with this line serving as his anchor, Lutz planned the creation of his own railroad through the Pinellas peninsula to compete with Plant's system. By 1911, he had constructed a railway line to Tarpon Springs that connected with the Tampa Northern Railroad at or near the end of the Gulf Pine route. He called his system the Tampa & Gulf Coast Railway and intended to extend it south all the way to St. Petersburg.

Unfortunately for Lutz, although St. Petersburg granted his business a city license, he was unable to acquire the necessary rights of way from landholders along this route. Refusing to give up, Lutz instead connected his track to a junction just northwest of the city of Tampa. A station was constructed at the head of the bay, leading to the establishment of the town of Oldsmar. The line then passed through Safety Harbor before continuing to Clearwater, Largo and Seminole and then terminating at St. Petersburg. In 1914, the project was completed. The local residents finally had their own rail route, and unlike the Orange Belt, it provided a direct link to Tampa. A branch line brought passengers north to Tarpon Springs and Port Richey.

The arrival of the train had an immediate impact on the burgeoning city. The rail link brought tourists to the popular mineral springs and allowed the farmers to ship their citrus and vegetable crops north without having to transport them over land to Largo. Building supplies could be delivered from Tampa. A station was built near Main Street to service the stop.

The city blossomed. By 1916, three passenger and three freight trains were arriving in Safety Harbor each day. In 1917, the slightly renamed Tampa & Gulf Coast Railroad was integrated into the Seaboard Air Line Railway system, which provided direct connections with most major cities in Florida. Although there was regular service, the trains didn't always stop right at the station. Often, passengers were required to walk up to a half mile along the tracks to board or to reach the stationhouse after disembarking.

In the mid-1920s, Seaboard began service of its "Orange Blossom Special," a luxury air-conditioned passenger train that connected Florida to Washington, New York, Boston and other northern cities on the East Coast during the winter tourist season. By 1928, seven trains left St. Petersburg on a daily basis along different routes, although two years later the *Evening Independent* reported that this schedule had been reduced to five. The Orange Blossom quickly gained in popularity; within a few years, professional baseball players such as Babe Ruth were known to use the line to get to spring training. Although many of the trains were express, for at least part of the time during its

Ready to ride the Seaboard. *Photo courtesy of Valerie Nolte.*

run the Orange Blossom stopped in Safety Harbor along its route. According to an article and periodic advertisements in the *Safety Harbor Herald* in 1936, several trains were scheduled to make regular local stops during that season. City residents could also travel to Miami for access to service up the east coast of Florida and beyond. By the mid-1940s, traffic at the station had increased to eight passenger and four freight trains daily.

The local railroad workers could almost be said to have their own community. For many years, they were given the opportunity to live with their families in unused boxcars owned by Seaboard that had been placed on the ground along the track and had been converted into homes. The boxcars stretched in a line leading about a half mile south of the entrance to the Brooklyn Heights neighborhood. Also, the workers were given vouchers known as "scrip" to be used to shop at the railroad store in Tampa, and they would often load up in trucks and make the trip together.

The train didn't come without risk, however. In 1926, a man named Curtis Sapp was found dead beside the track in Safety Harbor. He had been struck by a passing train. Then, two days after Christmas 1929, an automobile collided with the train at the Main Street crossing, but fortunately all passengers escaped serious injury. Nearly thirteen years later, in November 1942, Louise Pearce, the woman who decades earlier had driven the wagon to and from the Sylvan Abbey schoolhouse, was struck and killed by the train while trying to cross the tracks at Main Street. She was seventy-six at the time of her death.

Despite these incidents, the Main Street crossing continued to lack warning lights, and safety remained an issue. In early September 1953, a large truck carrying an estimated six thousand pounds of meat was struck by a southbound freight train at Main Street. The truck was split in two, and the meat was scattered one hundred feet down the tracks. Many longtime residents still vividly recall the townspeople picking up the meat strewn across the road and taking it home to be refrigerated. "It was gone within minutes," remembered David Nichols. The driver, a twenty-two-year-old Tampa man named Donald Amsler, was killed. Tragically, he was due to be married the following day.

One-time city commissioner William Blackshear recalled that another woman was struck and killed by the train at Main Street in the early 1960s. Around the same time, "[t]here was an emergency at Philippe Park, and as was the habit, the freight train had parked right on Main Street." Blackshear continued, "I don't know if the engineers had gotten out to get some coffee or something, [but they] just left the train right there, and the emergency vehicles couldn't get through." These events contributed to Blackshear's resolve to run for public office. Eventually, due in part to Blackshear's efforts, warning lights were finally installed at that crossing, and an alternate route into the city was created.

According to another longtime resident, some of the city's teenagers would occasionally hop onto the freight trains for a free ride to Clearwater,

Train at the Seaboard Depot, which faced east and was located south of Main Street just past Ninth Avenue, close to the current American Legion parking lot. *Photo courtesy of Valerie Nolte.*

getting off at the fruit plant across from the Kapok Tree Inn near where Ruth Eckerd Hall is today. "It was not that they were going anywhere," wrote Judi Baker. "It was just something fun to do." However, the practice was not altogether safe. Ms. Baker recalled that one young man injured his spine jumping off a train in Dunedin and became a paraplegic.

Between 1925 and 1963, the station agent was Glenn O. Petree, who worked without direct supervision and was widely lauded for his dedication and loyalty to the railroad. On that point, Petree's son Franklin recalled watching his father spend an entire weekend rebalancing the financial ledgers when they were off by a mere ten cents. Petree also served as the railroad telegraph operator.

From this station, boxcars full of citrus were shipped north for commercial distribution. It has been said that Pinellas County was at one time the largest exporter of citrus in the state, and the bulk of the business from the Safety Harbor station consisted of fruit shipped by local grove operators. The station was equipped with a system of rollers that was used to transport the citrus to the cars after being unloaded outside the other end of the terminal. Petree's granddaughter Valerie Nolte remembered climbing into empty crates as a child and riding along the system of rollers, the "closest thing we had to a carnival ride."

In October 1963, passenger service was ended at the Safety Harbor depot after business at the station declined. Two years later, in November 1965, the structure was demolished, providing a symbolic ending to fifty years of rail service to the city. The tracks are still used by CSX to ship freight to St. Petersburg.

SAFETY HARBOR'S BLACK COMMUNITY

A HIDDEN HISTORY

Chapter 13

Although limited, slivers of documentation offer a glimpse into Safety Harbor's African American history. Records from the U.S. census account for many people who worked as tenant farmers, farm laborers, "helpers," and turpentine laborers. Most of the early pioneers' stories have been lost, but what is known is that they faced many of the same circumstances as their white neighbors: harsh elements and hard work. They also shared a hope for a better future for their children. For example, in 1900, forty-one-year-old Jerry Folk and his thirty-five-year-old wife, Miley, lived in a rented house with their daughter and grandson in proximity to several of the town's future leaders. Mr. Folk could read but not write. Mrs. Folk could do neither, but their eighteen-year-old daughter, Irene Fulton, could both read and write.

There is no way to know exactly where most people lived according to today's Safety Harbor city limits, due to the absence of house numbers or identifying written accounts of precise locations of homes. This was especially true for the few early African Americans. Although the first black neighborhoods were platted just after the turn of the twentieth century, people working as laborers and "helpers" didn't always live away from their work. Most either rented houses from or lived with white employers.

In the years following the city's incorporation, a few small, modestly built homes began to rise north of Main Street, within a few blocks east and west of the railroad tracks. In the early 1920s, as told in Chapter 8, Charley and Amanda Smith brought their tiny daughter Goldie to Safety Harbor from

Georgia so that she could grow strong. In 2013, at age ninety-seven, Goldie (Smith) Banks recalled what Safety Harbor and their first home looked like:

> *When we came into Safety Harbor, there were no houses around here. It was a one-horse town. All these* [homes] *were just sand roads. My father was a builder. He built a little house for us. I think there was maybe two houses around here. They were nice little houses, but I don't think they had windows. We had sheets to divide the two rooms. We didn't have a bathroom. You had to go outside.*

Mr. Smith would wake up before sunrise to tend to his garden and then head to work for the remainder of the day. He laid some of the first bricks on Main Street. Mrs. Smith cleaned homes, and like her daughter, who would follow in her path years later, did not return to her own home until late evening. Goldie would also clean homes beginning at the age of twelve, and in addition she helped raise children, cooked, shopped and did much more for many families, including the Safety Harbor McMullens.

Both men and women found work in the citrus industry. There were jobs for farm workers. Many came to earn money picking grapefruit and oranges in some of Safety Harbor's and Clearwater's groves. After Seaboard came to town, men found jobs through the railroad. There were few career opportunities for either men or women at the time, and this caused many families to take on migrant work and travel north during the summer. Although some teaching positions did exist, it was almost impossible for women to find work other than domestic jobs.

Sundays were church days, and sometimes in the middle of the week people gathered to worship outdoors. Many Wednesday evenings, prayers and songs floated across town, touching ears throughout the whole city, the melodic sounds reaching across cultural lines.

Two churches served the early black community of Safety Harbor: Bethlehem Baptist Church, one of the city's oldest churches, and the African Methodist Episcopal Church. These provided centers for people to gather and socialize as well as worship. Although the *Safety Harbor Herald* perceived its clientele as mostly white, the paper occasionally advertised events for the black churches, such as concerts, speeches, mock trials and fundraisers. In such announcements, church leaders invited both black and white people to attend. The pastors likely felt discouraged at the lack of funding for their buildings, as their congregations were rich in community and culture but poor in financial resources.

SMALLPOX AND THE KU KLUX KLAN

Safety Harbor had few means, especially when disease or disaster struck, but in March 1926, when smallpox threatened Pinellas County, an estimated ten people in the black community were quarantined. The *Herald* had been advertising the boom of new growth and prosperity as if the city were experiencing a gold rush, but despite the exaggerated reports of development, many county leaders feared the threat of disease would discourage continued progress. About this epidemic, historian Eric Jarvis recently wrote:

> *The smallpox epidemic came quietly in late December 1925 and only became widespread in January and February 1926. While the disease spread to many parts of Florida, including Jacksonville and West Palm Beach, the largest number of cases and the most publicity about them occurred in Miami and Tampa. In those two cities health officials reacted more dramatically than elsewhere and generated the most significant amount of controversy over how to battle the outbreak. In both cities, the key issue involved the amount of reporting that should be allowed, since any adverse press coverage had the potential to damage the economy.*

Although the *Herald* reported that "[n]o new cases of small pox developed in the city," Pinellas County helped to fund an emergency hospital to be set up in an area occupied by Safety Harbor's black residents. The "hospital" consisted of three army tents: one for women, one for men and one for attendants and cooks. The tents were equipped with cots, mattresses and bedding and were described as being "more comfortable than the average home of the colored people."

It was believed the disease was brought to the city from an unnamed source through clothing sent to be laundered by a woman in the black community. Safety Harbor's Dr. Edwards assisted the district health officer, Dr. Coulter, to immunize and isolate cases of smallpox, although the *Herald* reported, "Several of the colored people have said the doctors did not know what they were talking about and that it was simply chicken pox."

Whether the individual cases were indeed only chicken pox or actually smallpox is not known. Nor is it known whether the cases were severe or mild. The gender, ages and occupations of the people quarantined are lost to the years, but the frustration of the unnamed patients is apparent in the following 1926 *Safety Harbor Herald* account, as are the horrible consequences should the quarantined patients have chosen not to cooperate:

Sheriff Booth established guards to patrol around the tents, two men well armed, on 12 hour shifts….No one is allowed to enter or leave the hospital grounds except the doctor or those who have the right to do so…Dr. Edwards had some unpleasant experiences when he went to vaccinate a few of these people. And the warning is sounded here and now that any more of the foolishness will be dealt with in a manner approved appropriate to the case. It might be that the Ku Klux Klan will be asked to take a hand in the matter and if the white robed men come there will be action sure enough. The Herald is told that the prime motive of the clan [sic] is to have law and order enforced at any cost and if it is necessary to chain some of the violators to a pine tree and administer the punishment necessary it will be done. This applies to the white people as well as the colored…the members have visited Safety Harbor before and if they have found the city once they can do it again.

Although the city was small, the Ku Klux Klan had a known presence in Safety Harbor in the 1920s and 1930s. Mention of the KKK or "members of the hooded order" appeared again in the *Safety Harbor Herald* in 1927, stating that approximately fifty members arrived at the (white) Methodist church to donate money to the building fund. Other evidence of their public appearance is a firsthand account by Clyde Rigsby, a Safety Harbor native. Along with his twin brother, Claude, Mr. Rigsby was an active member of the white community who was born in and grew up in the house that is now the location of the Safety Harbor Art and Music Center:

We were scared. My folks didn't like it. They didn't believe in treating the black people like they [the KKK] was. We come out there and we could hear marching. We could see about sixty of them with white hoods. We knew who they was 'cause you could see their pants sticking out.

There are no further known articles documenting the Ku Klux Klan in Safety Harbor until 1952, when a political rally in the city brought an unexpected number of people, as well as propaganda. The *St. Petersburg Times* reported that "[a]t the termination of the rally, spectators found their automobiles plastered with Klan literature and notices urging Bill Hendricks for governor." It is not known when the KKK's presence declined or whether there was any effort to stop it in later years, but it did take years for similar ideals to die off.

As for the smallpox epidemic, there has been no documentation found regarding its final outcome in Safety Harbor.

A FORGOTTEN CEMETERY

Many families, both black and white, suffered the death of young children. In 1937, the *Safety Harbor Herald* reported such a tragic loss:

> *Sunday night three children of Jim and Bertha Campbell, colored, were playing beside their cabin, located near the Sylvan Abbey cemetery. They had built a fire in the open and as it was not burning well enough to suit their childish fancies the thought occurred to them to use some kerosene. The father and mother had retired. They had a can containing about five gallons of kerosene. The oil exploded scattering fire over the children. Jim immediately rushed into the yard and began to tear the clothing from the oldest girl, fifteen years, who was trying to pour water on herself to put out the fire. He also tore the clothing from his son of ten and in so doing was quite badly burned himself. The other girl, Bessie Mae[,] was not so seriously burned and will recover.*
>
> *A white person was passing by and he took the children in his car to the Morton Plant Hospital in Clearwater where they received treatment. The oldest girl, Bertha, died at 1:10 Tuesday morning while the boy, James, died at 10:00 o'clock. The little girl, Bessie Mae, five years old, is well on the road to recovery. Funeral services will be held Sunday with burial in the Safety Harbor colored cemetery.*

The Safety Harbor African American Cemetery is located in a residential neighborhood at 2698 South Drive, now considered to be within Clearwater's boundaries due to land annexations that have occurred over time. Many graves are unmarked, but the earliest gravestone belongs to Samuel E. Swann, who died in 1896 when he was only a few months old.

Early in the twentieth century, the land was designated for continued use as a resting place for the local African American community by Solomon Smith Coachman, who purchased the former McMullen groves in 1902. Sometime during the Depression, the Coachman family lost the property. Eventually, the surrounding neighborhood, including the land used for the graveyard, was purchased by Alfred and Louisa Ehle, who created a subdivision, leaving Lot 15 empty for its continued use as the cemetery. According to Safety Harbor resident Yvonne Hedgeman, some of the graves were relocated when the subdivision was built. In 1951, the Ehles deeded Lot 15 to "St. Vincent Helping Hand Society." Then, in 1953, the land was sold to the "Safety Harbor Colored Community" for one dollar.

Mrs. Hedgeman said that there are so many graves on the property that people may be buried on top of one another. Although in disrepair, when funds are available the cemetery is still cared for by many who remember loved ones buried there. Since the graves are mostly unmarked, names and locations of specific burials were often remembered only by family members and friends and sometimes noted on pieces of paper that were only temporarily secured at the grave sites. The locations of the Campbell children are not known, as there are no headstones that bear their names. The cemetery was used as late as the 1970s.

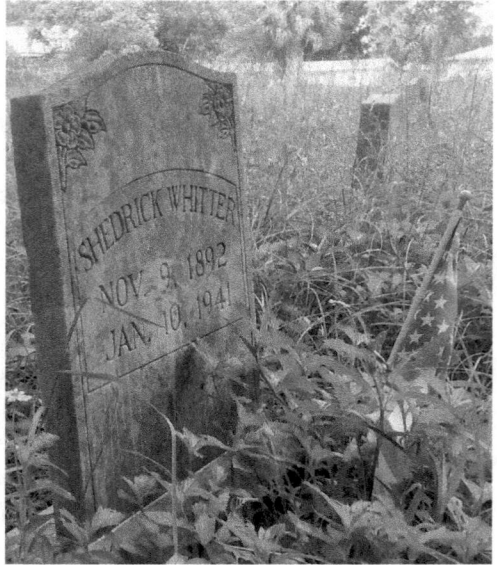

Gravestone of Shedrick Whitter, born November 9, 1892, died January 10, 1941. *Photo by Warren Firschein.*

Ingenuity, Leadership and Powerful Voices

William Blackshear came to Safety Harbor in 1947, when he was in the sixth grade. Like other Safety Harbor children, Blackshear enjoyed the area's wilderness and the freedom to explore. He and his friends would go to the area that is now Philippe Park to collect arrowheads and look at the mounds. "But that's not really what we went for," he said. "There were wild grapes that could drive you mad. They were big purple things and around July the grapes grew on old thick vines in the trees, all the way down Bayshore."

Young Blackshear moved away, but as an adult, he returned with his wife and children. A development at the black community of Lincoln Highlands was offering brand-new two- and three-bedroom homes for around $8,000. The Blackshears purchased a house on Tenth Avenue North and were excited about their new home.

Although Mr. Blackshear lived in Safety Harbor at a time when neither he nor other black people were allowed to participate in simple pleasures such as watching a movie in the local theater or eating in one of the restaurants, he spoke of the town as a place where he experienced kindness. "I never felt out of place. I guess because I moved from a southern city to a southern city," he said. "With Safety Harbor, I always felt that it was kind of calm. I don't remember anybody being ugly."

But he does recall a growing frustration that continued to build, as Mr. Blackshear soon realized that there were things lacking in their neighborhood. He would often complain to an older friend at General Electric's Pinellas Peninsula Plant, where he worked in advanced production on the Atomic Energy Commission contract. "I would just sit and grumble," he said. "Until she said, 'Why don't you do something about it?'"

The Blackshears had difficulty finding daycare for their two smallest children, not yet in school. The lack of daycare services for African Americans became a key issue that many families faced as well. After becoming president of the Lincoln School PTA and chairman of the Lincoln Highland Home Improvement Committee, Mr. Blackshear learned a lot about solving community problems. "My wife took the kids every day to Clearwater. We wanted our own daycare, so we started another organization, the Lincoln Nursery Association."

The committee appealed to a community service organization and within a year they had their daycare. Blackshear didn't stop there, though. By organizing committees, he had already become familiar with public speaking. He also made connections with town leaders, who soon encouraged him to run for office.

At age twenty-nine, on November 10, 1964, William Blackshear was elected as city commissioner by twenty-two votes. He was the first African American person to hold a political office in Safety Harbor and possibly the first in the state of Florida since the end of Reconstruction.

In 1965, President Johnson signed the Voting Rights Act. "There were blacks being elected to office all over the south," Blackshear said. "He invited all of us to the White House—all thirty to forty. It was wonderful."

William Blackshear, Safety Harbor's first African American commissioner, being sworn into office in 1964 with new mayor George McGonegal. *Photo courtesy of William Blackshear.*

Many people in the Brooklyn and Lincoln areas wanted better living conditions. One issue that plagued the community was the poor state of the roads. None of the roads in Lincoln Highlands, Lincoln Heights or the Brooklyn area were paved, not even Ninth Avenue, a road frequented by city workers and residents alike. Due to the condition of the roads there was no garbage or postal service into the Brooklyn subdivision. Although America was changing, Safety Harbor was still burdened by its long history of debt.

During his time as city commissioner, Mr. Blackshear worked to get a crossing signal installed on Main Street and an alternate route to Philippe Park. He also wanted Ninth Avenue paved and city limits defined: "We wanted to do some annexation, but it was too late. The idea for annexing vacant land was that you were doing so for the future, for taxes, but we lost out on that. We were still paying off bankruptcy bonds."

Mr. Blackshear had hoped to bring the Brooklyn subdivision into city limits. It was one of those undefined areas outside the borders over which Safety Harbor had jurisdiction. Not only would the city have benefitted from the additional taxes from places that were annexed, but also neighborhoods such as Brooklyn, whose residents were among the poorest people in Pinellas County, could have had city services.

After the conclusion of his term in office, William Blackshear and his family moved away. Later in his career, he partnered with Cleveland Johnson to establish the *Challenger*, a weekly St. Petersburg newspaper for and about the African American community. In 2008, Mr. Blackshear was selected to act as grand marshal for the Safety Harbor Holiday Parade. He now resides in Dunnellon with his wife, Betty.

Water for Brooklyn

Most of the people living in Brooklyn subdivision homes had access to shallow wells until 1962, when an outbreak of infant diarrhea was blamed on contaminated water. All but two of the wells were condemned. Pinellas County studied the feasibility of bringing water to the subdivision but considered the $19,000 cost not economically practical for the number of potential customers who would be added.

Brooklyn residents obtained water from a spigot provided by the city and carried it home in buckets. Finally, in 1967, an organization calling itself

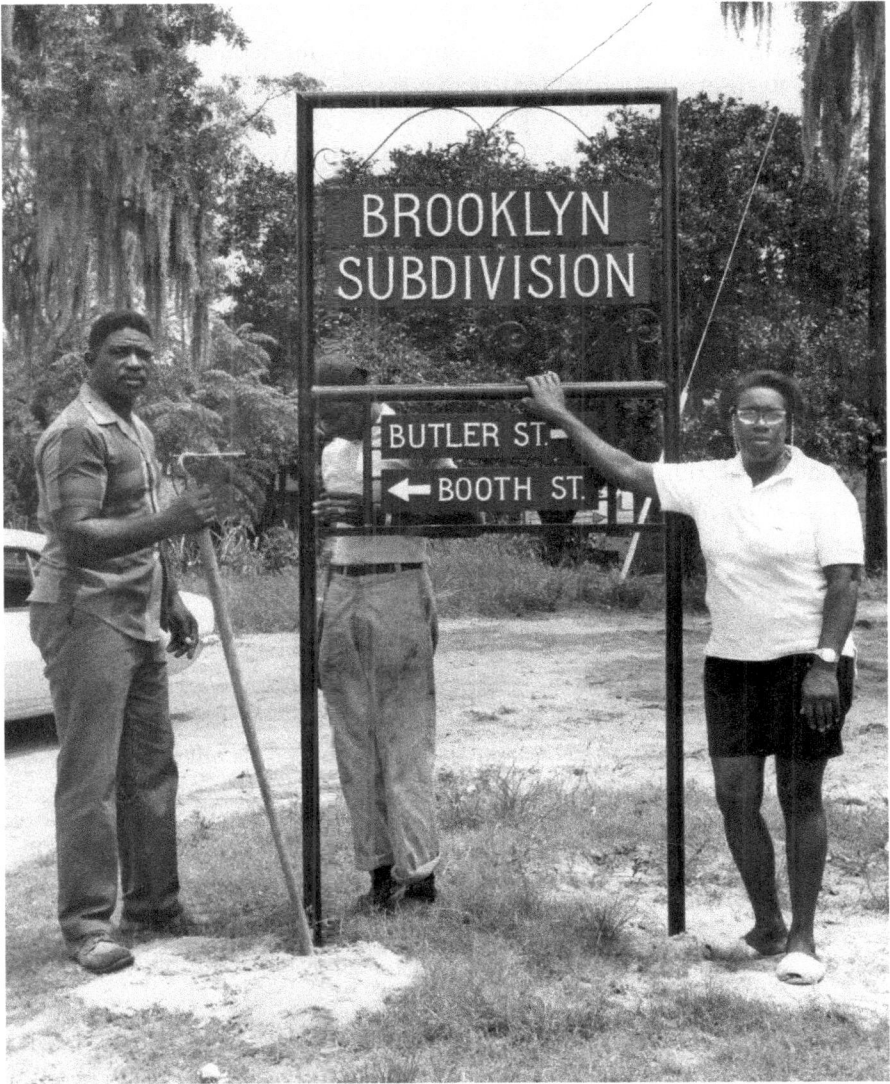

Residents of the Brooklyn subdivision fought hard to gain services. *From left:* Johnny Salph, Charles Allen and Mrs. T.L. Fort, 1968. *Photo by Mike Fleischer/*St. Petersburg Times.

Harbor Opportunity Promotion Efforts (HOPE) took an interest in the citizens. HOPE got Safety Harbor to agree to allow the county to tap into the city's water main at Seventh Street and Ninth Avenue North, approximately five hundred feet from the subdivision.

The *St. Petersburg Times* reported, "Realizing the plight of Brooklyn residents, the city offered the water to the county at the city's cost with no extra charge for transmission. Although this offer reduced the cost from $19,000 to approximately $4,000 for water service to Brooklyn, [the] County again refused the project."

In 1968, the Community Action Neighbors (CAN) was organized. The group urged Safety Harbor's City Commission to assist it in getting the Pinellas County Commission to help, but Pinellas County still did not act.

A citizens' campaign was organized, and $2,500 was raised for the water project, but there was still the cost of the water line to consider. Two contractors in Clearwater stepped in and agreed to donate their services, and the city commission worked with the Seaboard Coast Line Railroad (the successor to the Seaboard Air Line Railway), which for months had not agreed to allow the city to install a water line under the railroad tracks.

Finally, in 1969, most of the Brooklyn subdivision had water, but years later, in 1978, an article appeared in the *St. Petersburg Times* describing a three-block area with about twenty cardboard and plywood hovels:

> *There are no indoor toilet facilities here, no running water, no heat, frequently no electricity, no telephones, no fire hydrants...Children do not play here—most of the stinking burned-out shacks and hovels are inhabited by disabled, middle-aged black persons...It is an area shunned by younger black families, many of whom live on the other side of the railroad tracks less than 100 feet across 9th [Avenue] North in the modern concrete block homes on the paved streets of Lincoln Heights.*

From Brooklyn and Lincoln: Leaders

As a child in the Panhandle of Florida in the 1940s and 1950s, Luella Horne and her eight siblings were raised by a single mother. Luella picked cotton and tobacco and shucked peanuts to help earn money, and she didn't own a new article of clothing until high school. She had seen how difficult life had been for her mother and knew she wanted to finish school and eventually own a home. Years later, married and with a small son, Luella (Horne) Myrick worked for Pinellas High School as a baker. In 1961, she found a second job, and she and her husband began saving for the down payment on a new home being built in Lincoln Highlands. Mrs. Myrick said that she would bring her son to the property every Sunday after church to watch the progress of their home's construction.

At first the new Lincoln Highlands homeowners took care of their properties and their pride in ownership showed, but years later, problems arose. Junk cars, boats and trash littered the neighborhood. There were no sidewalks or paved streets, and drug deals became rampant. "Every time one group got cleaned up, another would come," Mrs. Myrick said. Although at first she felt intimidated, Mrs. Myrick began attending city commission meetings. She organized neighborhood committees and wrote letters to Sheriff Rice, and in 1982 she got the attention she had wanted. Not too long after, partially due to Mrs. Myrick's persistence, Sheriff Rice arrested twenty-three people.

Like Mrs. Myrick, many Lincoln and Brooklyn residents began to take a more active role in the improvement of their neighborhoods. In the mid-1990s, a group of citizens formed a coalition to address the issues that they realized were stemming from the underlying problems of substance abuse. The group applied for and received a grant from the Juvenile Welfare Board to establish a neighborhood center. Now, the Mattie Williams Neighborhood Family Center, located on Ninth Avenue North and Martin Luther King Street North, is a nonprofit organization that provides support services to community members in need.

The center's namesake, Mattie Williams, was like many women in the community. Although she had not been a resident of Brooklyn or Lincoln for many years, she reached out to those in need, no matter where they lived, by donating time, offering compassion and doing whatever else she could to help.

The vibrant history of Safety Harbor's black community is proof that the patience and determination of the past generations has allowed for a better future from which today's generation, as well as future generations, will benefit.

Chapter 14

FROM WORLD WAR II TO THE END
OF THE MILLENNIUM

THE CHANGING COMMUNITY

O n December 7, 1941, the U.S. naval base at Pearl Harbor was attacked by a surprise military strike conducted by the Imperial Japanese Navy, and Safety Harbor prepared for war. The city was divided into four zones, and local men were appointed as wardens to defend each section of the city.

Mayor L.H. Zinsser formed a temporary committee to protect the community and a second committee to appoint a volunteer firefighting force. Others attended frequent fire drills to prepare for emergency. A woman named Mrs. Eleanor Davis was asked to teach classes on first aid work. *Safety Harbor Herald* editor A.E. Shower wrote, "It is very nice to notice the unity prevailing in the defense work in the community and all are going about it just as if there was not another group like it in the United States and that the winning of the war really depended on what they do. That is the right spirit and the spirit that will win."

In compliance with the national defense program, Safety Harbor held its first blackout drill less than a month later. Residents were instructed to turn off all lights, take shelter and stay inside, since outdoor areas were considered to be the most dangerous. Those who found it necessary to drive automobiles during the drill were instructed to pull to the side of the road and turn off the engine and the lights. Later into the war, drivers were required to blacken their headlights with paint. Once again, Shower adopted a fatherly tone:

We must do all we can to beat the Axis powers. Better be dead than to live with them as our rulers. If they win there will never be any freedom left in the world. What are we going to do about it? Naturally we are going to obey all orders and by so doing help democracy to live and help that we can have freedom in the years to come, if not for ourselves, then for the oncoming generation.

Local children also took part in the war effort by buying Savings War Stamps, often after marching as a group to the post office. Although the marches were organized for the white students, children and teachers at the all-black Lincoln Heights School also wanted to support the troops, and on at least one occasion memorialized by the *St. Petersburg Times*, they "followed right along right after the children of the Safety Harbor white school," marking the effort as "100 per cent [t]he entire population of Safety Harbor."

By 1942, the U.S. government was urging farm families to produce more milk, eggs, peanuts and vegetables. Many in Safety Harbor planted Victory Gardens, blunting the impact of food and gas rationing. Everyone made do despite restrictions on many products.

Of Safety Harbor's approximately 700 residents, 114 white men and women and between 25 and 30 black men served in the armed forces. Parents, sweethearts and family members eagerly awaited news from overseas. Letters such as the following were mailed directly to the *Herald* and printed for everyone to read:

> *Div. 6A Eugene E. Graef*
> *U.S.S._____,*
> *c/o Fleet Post Office*
> *San Francisco, Calif.,*
> *Nov. 29, 1942*
> *Chamber of Commerce,*
> *Safety Harbor, Florida.*
>
> *Dear Sirs;*
> *I send my greatest appreciation for the thoughtfulness, you the people of Safety Harbor, for remembering all the sons of that swell city. It has been a long time since I last saw it, a little over three years. I thought that by now the whole town had forgotten even my memory. It is nice to know we are fighting for such a worthy cause as to keep the spirit of friendship and freedom with us forever. I think I speak for all men in my position when I say we appreciate*

everything you do for all the men in the armed service. Someday we will return to Safety Harbor and find a proud and decent city in which to settle and raise our families to be the kind of people we are fighting for.

Sincerely yours,
Eugene E. Graef

In 1943, the city received word that the U.S. Marine Auxiliary would come to the area to train. Many of the servicemen stationed nearby were housed at the Alden Apartment Building, which had been designated as barracks. These troops became a part of the community, if only for a short time, and at least a few of Safety Harbor's young women found husbands from among their number.

As the war dragged on, more and more women were called to action at home, not just by signing up for noncombatant positions but also by filling roles in the community previously held exclusively by men. One of these pioneers was Mary Ingersoll, who in 1944 became the first woman to serve in the city government when she was appointed to the job of city manager.

In July 1944, the city organized an American Legion post to serve the needs of those returning home from all forms of military service. It was named the Lawton-Harrington Post, in honor of Carl Lawton and Cecil Harrington, Safety Harbor's first casualties of war in both World War I and World War II, respectively. By the end of World War II, Safety Harbor had experienced the loss of five men.

POSTWAR SAFETY HARBOR: TIME STANDS STILL

The late 1940s and early 1950s were a time of postwar recovery for most of America, but as veterans returned, Safety Harbor probably looked the same as it had before the war. Jobs were scarce, and as longtime resident David Nichols recounted, many men spent their time in the bars or congregated on the curb outside Barron's Drugstore on the corner of Main Street and Philippe Parkway, the location where Crispers now stands. "Rednecks and poor people," Nichols said. "It was a rough-and-tumble town full of blight and drunks. People wanted it to grow, but city fathers weren't doing anything to let it grow." Safety Harbor's exposure to the outside world was limited. "Even radio reception was bad," Nichols added.

Safety Harbor residents had all they needed in town. Hardware, feed for animals, groceries and medicine could be found along Main Street. "When I was a young girl, we had several grocery stores," recalled B.J. Lehman, who has owned her flower shop at 101 Main Street for over fifty years.

> *Where Brady's* [Barbecue] *is now was a grocery store, where the post office is now and where Captain's Pizza was, they were all grocery stores. There was also Twitchell's at Tenth and Main* [south side], *and over where the dry cleaner is, there was a store there too.*

Although the days of carriages were long gone when she was a child, she also remembers a detail carried over from her grandfather Ward McMullen's generation: "Curbs were once two-layered so the ladies could step out of the carriage and onto the curb. The curbs were probably twelve or fifteen inches high. People would tether their horses right outside."

There wasn't much to do for entertainment in Safety Harbor, although for a time, a youth center served the community's kids, who could go to a dance, play games or enjoy occasional organized activities. As they did in generations past, kids rode around town on their bicycles, swam in the bay and until it was dammed, rowed small boats down Alligator Creek. Some stayed out all day, eating what grew. This tradition persisted. Christine Purvis recently recalled carrying a saltshaker in her pocket years later so she could eat fresh homegrown tomatoes from a friendly neighbor's garden when biking through town. At times, the young folks continued the time-honored custom of cooking chicken and rice pilleau outside in a large pot, especially when they had plenty of friends to share it with. If someone had a radio, there might even be a lazy afternoon listening to music at the dock.

During the late winter and early spring of 1947, plans were underway to dam Alligator Creek and turn it into a freshwater lake. The irrigation project drained an area of approximately five thousand acres of land, five

Alligator Lake was a prime fishing location after being dammed. *Photo courtesy of Valerie Nolte.*

Sunshine Downs in Oldsmar, January 19, 1953: a win for Safety Harbor's Alabama Bell. *Photo courtesy of Safety Harbor Museum and Cultural Center.*

hundred of which were very low and prone to mosquitoes. The area was converted to a lake covering one hundred acres, with a seven-hundred-foot dam. By its completion, Alligator Lake was just under six feet deep and stocked with fish.

After thirteen years without a local track, horse racing resumed at Sunshine Park in Oldsmar in 1947. This meant more visitors to Safety Harbor's hotels and businesses. The *Safety Harbor Herald* reported that every available room, cottage and apartment in both Oldsmar and Safety Harbor had been rented in January 1947 "by the racetrack people and the friends of racing."

The racing season corresponded roughly to the months that the spa was operational. During the summer months, the spa put paper in the windows, and the city essentially shut down to visitors. "By June, grass was all through the bricks," said William Blackshear. "Jobs closed too. Now you had to exist over the summer with no work. You went to nature. If you could eat, you were okay. There were a lot of little farms around Safety Harbor. You could grow your own and hunt."

After Philippe Park was established in 1948, two years after the death of landowner Thomas Palmer, the grounds became a place for children to explore and search for Tocobaga arrowheads. In the coming years, the park would become a location for evening performances that celebrated the area and made the past come alive.

A ROUGH-AND-TUMBLE TOWN

At some point, the city started to be referred to as "Whiskey Harbor," and for good reason. Moonshine was common in the 1940s and continued being discreetly produced for years afterward in wooded areas on private land.

Looking back, it might be hard to imagine that Safety Harbor was known as a place where drunks stumbled out of bars late at night and fights broke out often. However, many remember empty buildings in disrepair, a "redneck" mentality and extensive drug and alcohol use. For a time, the city had a bad reputation and deserved it. Bars were frequented by many. The after-work crowd stopped in for a couple of drinks. Others stayed into the night, with some getting in trouble with the law. Not coincidentally, church attendance declined.

Two of the popular bars, the Harbor Bar and the Tavern, were situated close to each other along Philippe Parkway. Even long after the beginning of the civil rights era, the Tavern allowed only white people in the main room; black men and women were required to order their drinks in a separate room, which they could get to only by going through the storeroom. There was a little window—nothing more than a hole in the wall—through which the owner would check on his black customers.

"This place got really bad," Joe Samnik recently recalled, speaking of the Tavern. "Virgil [the owner] got his shotgun out whenever there was trouble. And there was trouble: fights, robberies, drug deals. You name it." Customers called it the Shooting Gallery.

The following excerpt from the *St. Petersburg Times* described one such incident:

At about 7:30 p.m. Friday night when the argument reached a point where Goth reportedly had a butcher knife and Reed a gun, Safety Harbor Police said they were on their way. Although they arrived minutes after the fight started, a bystander, Maude Bascome, already had been shot in the shoulder.

Main Street during the 1970s "Whiskey Harbor" days. *Photo courtesy of Heritage Village Archives and Library.*

Today, the parcel of land used by the once-rowdy bar is occupied by the Safety Harbor Public Library.

During the later years of the 1950s, Safety Harbor appeared to be coming apart at the seams. Turnover among city employees was rampant, particularly among the police force. When patrolman Glenn Gammage resigned in March 1957 after just one month on the job, he was the fifth patrolman to quit in less than a year, leaving Chief John Anderson, who had himself been recently hired, as the sole member of the city's police department. Anderson became embroiled in controversy several weeks later amid allegations that he had failed to file required reports with the city commission.

In mid-April 1957, the hammer of small-town politics fell on the city. The mayor at the time was Ben Downs—the same Ben Downs who, as a young teenager almost thirty years before, struck early pioneer "Keeter" Booth with a car while Booth was riding a horse to a boxing exhibition. At the conclusion of a city commission meeting that was described as "violent," Mayor Downs unexpectedly announced, "I am going to declare an emergency. I am going to fire the police chief." After new commissioner Howard Grace asked what he meant by an "emergency," Downs replied, "The condition of the city" and maintained that the city charter gave him authority over the police force in times of emergency. Also ousted was city building inspector Newton Coler. It was later reported that Downs had charged Chief Anderson with using profanity in talking to a youth accused of being a troublemaker, but it seems unlikely that this relatively minor infraction could have been the impetus for Mayor Downs's actions. But just one day later, Circuit Court Judge John U. Bird ruled that Downs did not have the authority to fire any city officials except during a vast emergency such as riots or great disasters and voided the firings.

On April 17, the commissioners voted to end the "emergency," and the two employees were reinstated. Two weeks later, on May 2, Police Chief Anderson resigned anyway, effective May 16. In June, Coler was fired a second time as the electrical inspector and allowed to hand in his resignation as the building inspector.

Following this fiasco, Safety Harbor was widely ridiculed for its politics by neighboring cities, and a recall effort against Mayor Downs was initiated. But Downs remained unabashed. In August 1957, when new police chief B.D. Samuels was hired, Mayor Downs refused to give up the free telephone that he had installed in his home when he was acting as temporary police chief, claiming that he was entitled to a free telephone even though the telephone company advised that the four free phones provided to the city were meant for the fire and police departments and city hall.

Later in the year, Mayor Downs successfully weathered the special recall election by a vote of 230 to 154, and he was even reelected in 1958. However, the damage to the reputation of the city had been done.

In 1959, as the city tried to repair its image, a major crime earned a lasting spot in local lore by targeting the inviolate Safety Harbor Resort and Spa. In the middle of a night in early March, three masked men brandishing revolvers crept through the "darkened hallways of the plush winter resort." Upon reaching the spa's office, they bound, blindfolded and gagged night watchman Pierce Owens and telephone operator Helen Rowe and proceeded to rob the safe of an estimated $200,000 in cash, checks and jewelry. The perpetrators were as stylish as they were daring, as they were reported to have been wearing "white yachting caps and blue jackets...in matching Dick Tracy comic book style." The thieves appear to never have been identified. Coming on the heels of the political debacle of just a few years earlier, it was a sad but fitting end to a long decade in a declining city.

THE END OF AN ERA AND MANY NEW BEGINNINGS

The man who wrote hundreds of articles as editor of the *Safety Harbor Herald*, Alva Ernest Shower, passed away in 1961 at the age of eighty-four. The town was saddened by the loss of someone it considered to be one of the city's most influential pioneers. Since his retirement in 1957, there had been a noticeable difference in the way in which the town was represented by the *Herald*. Shower's son Franklin had been editor since A.E.'s retirement and continued with the publication, but there was a noticeable change in the style of the paper. Items were less personal in nature, and the "local happenings" columns and other community news that had been a staple of the newspaper since its inception gradually vanished.

Despite the difficulties of the postwar era, there were still those who worked toward bettering the city. One of these people was Dr. Baranoff, the owner of the Safety Harbor Resort and Spa. Almost immediately upon his arrival in Safety Harbor, Dr. Baranoff became involved in a variety of community organizations and provided funding for several significant civic projects. In 1946, after learning that the community was in need of a larger library, he purchased two lots on the corner of Fifth Avenue and Second Street North (currently the location of Harborside Studios) and donated them for that purpose. He also purchased the old police court building as a home for the Safety Harbor American Legion Post, made the down payment and then paid off the mortgage. Baranoff also provided use of the spa facilities free of charge for all types of activities, most notably to the local Jewish community for meetings and fundraising activities.

Over time, participation increased in Girl Scout and Boy Scout troops, Kiwanis and the Garden Club and other community and social organizations. Often in the 1950s and 1960s, carnivals, temporary skating rinks, mechanical rides, craft contests, performances, historical society reenactments, cultural displays and other events would take place on the pier or in an empty lot across the street that would later become the site of Crispers. As they do today, city residents came out in great numbers to celebrate the culture and history of Safety Harbor.

In 1962, the Jacobsen Trailer Plant became a welcome addition to the Safety Harbor workforce. That same year, a man named David Lewis purchased the drugstore at 946 Main Street from Roger McCaskill. Lewis and his pharmacy became a beloved one-stop shop for many of Safety Harbor's citizens for many years. "In the '80s," explained longtime resident Laura Dent, "we would go to get medication for our children at his pharmacy, and when we did not have enough to buy it, he would take out his little black book and put our name down. Then he would say, 'When you have the money, come and pay.' I was so thankful for that. I heard he did it for many."

TURNING A CITY AROUND

By 1976, Safety Harbor was once again in a state of deep financial crisis. The campaigns for the open position of city commissioner that year focused on the need for a tighter budget. An audit for the 1974–75 fiscal year showed that the city's expenditures exceeded its revenue by $70,000. Moreover, Safety Harbor had recently borrowed $150,000, and a $300,000 bond issue was set to mature in only eleven months.

The abolition of the police department in 1976 saved the city an estimated annual expense of $80,000, but the calls for civic change and community improvement continued to grow. Problems that had festered since the city's bankruptcy during the Depression were reaching a boiling point. Jewel McKeon, who became the first female president of the Chamber of Commerce in 1979, remembers the silence of Main Street that seemed to last for many years. "If there were three cars from the chamber to the railroad tracks, you'd be surprised," she said.

Forward-thinking people worked to improve the community. In an effort to preserve the city's culture and history, septuagenarian Jim Miller volunteered his time to "spur growth of the museum," reaching out to the community and asking Safety Harbor residents to take an active interest in the past. Under Miller's leadership, the city's museum expanded its exhibits and increased its educational programs. In 1981, Miller arranged the signing of a peace treaty with the United Lenape Band as a part of a ceremony to reinter skeletal remains of a Tocobaga mother and child discovered two years earlier. The treaty ensured that the burial site, located on the museum's property, would never be disturbed or desecrated. It was believed to be the first treaty between American Indians and people of European descent in Pinellas County since the agreement negotiated by Pedro Menéndez de Avilés in 1567.

While Miller was trying to preserve the past, the city was ready to move on and look toward the future. In 1981, the historic Silver Dome building was demolished after it was declared unsafe and not suitable for renovation. But the city was in transition, and the seeds of Safety Harbor's art community were planted when Lois Spencer and her husband helped to organize Safety Harbor's first arts and crafts show.

Mrs. Spencer, who would later establish an antique store on Main Street, proved to have a knack for coordinating large events. She became involved with the museum, hoping to help raise funds, and hosted annual antique shows to bring people together. Safety Harbor's first Seafood Festival was a huge success in the mid-1980s as well. "I had ten seafood vendors," she said. "We had room for seventy-five vendors, and through the years, we never changed the fee. We wanted people to come out."

New parks were also created. Former constable and police chief Claude Rigsby, upon his retirement as mayor, recounted, "That [John] Wilson fellow who owns all the package liquor stores wanted to build on a Main Street lot he owned. He was too close to a church, so we wouldn't give him a permit. The only other suitable location needed a Commission zoning variance. So we let him know the Commission would be more favorable to the variance if we had a park downtown. So he gave us [a] site he owned [for a park]." While some may view this action as an abuse of power, John Wilson Park has endured, and today it is a gathering spot where people of all ages sit on the grass, relax and listen to music performances in the city gazebo.

In 1985, Hurricane Elena affected the region and caused extensive damage in the amount of nearly $4 million to Safety Harbor. Yet what affected the citizens the most was the loss of the pier. However, its reconstruction took less than a year.

Sadly, in the summer of 1986, a car was driven onto the newly renovated pier and set on fire by an unknown arsonist. Afterward, Safety Harbor's fire chief, Jay Stout, remarked, "It's a strike out against the whole community." He echoed what many people felt: it was a personal offense.

Safety Harbor was ready to turn the corner. New development commenced throughout the city. The simmering spirit of the early pioneers rallied the community, and by the millennium, the city was ready for further positive change. It would not take long for residents and tourists alike to take notice.

Chapter 15

CIVIC ORGANIZATIONS

SAFETY HARBOR'S POLICE DEPARTMENT, FIRE DEPARTMENT AND MORE

HISTORY OF THE SAFETY HARBOR POLICE FORCE

Soon after Pinellas County was created in 1912, a sheriff was elected, and five separate justice of the peace districts were established, each with its own constable.[8] Along with the communities of Oldsmar and Bayview, Safety Harbor was included in District 3, which extended from Lake Tarpon to near the St. Petersburg-Clearwater International Airport. The district was located mostly east of U.S. 19, although a section crossed the highway to include portions of Clearwater and Largo. Prior to 1912, the law was enforced by the Hillsborough County Sheriff's Office, although the frequency with which duties were performed on the Pinellas peninsula during those early years is unknown.

---

8. The purpose of having a constable was to have a policeman readily available in each area to quickly investigate trouble. Their duties, spelled out in Florida state statutes, allowed them to make arrests and investigations, serve warrants and other legal documents, serve as bailiffs in the justice of the peace courts and perform related functions. They also mediated family or neighborhood disputes and helped distressed persons. Constables worked under a "fee system" paid out of what was collected from court costs and were therefore paid based on the number of arrests. However, if a case was dismissed for insufficient cause, no fees would be collected, so there was no incentive to pad arrest numbers by arresting innocent individuals. The advantage to sparsely populated areas like Safety Harbor was that they could have the services of a constable without having to pay a full-time salary. The position of constable was abolished in 1972.

Locally, minor offenses (mostly driving violations) were handled by the City or Mayor's Court, which appears to have been established soon after the incorporation of the city in 1917. A log book from the Mayor's Court from the city's early years, on display at the Safety Harbor Museum and Cultural Center, preserves a record of those infractions and the resulting fines. Those issuing citations included Officers Pearce, Branning, Fisher, Davis, Wilson, Cook, and Lillie, but other than their names, all records of these individuals and the circumstances under which they were appointed to this role have been lost to time.

The extent of more significant police activity in the young city is unclear, but in 1926, the same year of the alleged smallpox outbreak, there was reason enough for the city to order the installation of two jail cells. As reported by the *Safety Harbor Herald*, "those who are not in the notion of obeying the laws of the city will have an opportunity to think it over." The cells were initially set up in the city hall. Although convenient, they were only short-term holding cells; offenders requiring longer stays were transferred to the county jail.

For a number of years, District 3 had been without a constable "due to the lack of business," meaning that it wasn't profitable to holders of the position. Starting in the early 1930s, a man named John Strickland served in the position for several years, until replaced by Percy Vasbinder in 1936.

Vasbinder, who became a dominant law presence in the area for the next twenty-four years, was born in Richmond, Virginia, in 1893. The World War I veteran was a tall, lanky man, missing several fingers on one hand and often used the nubs of those fingers against a person's ribcage to make a point. Thora Carroll grew up in Safety Harbor and remembers him as a strict lawman:

> He was a rough man, not afraid of anyone, and lots of people respected him for that. He was my dad's friend and if my dad had broken the law, Percy would have taken him to jail. It was said Percy would have arrested his own mother if she broke the law.

Bobby Morrow was more concise: "He was a real badass."

For the growing city, the constable's and sheriff's services as the sole providers of law enforcement were insufficient, and at some point Safety Harbor created its own police department to handle more serious crime than that enforced by the officers of the Mayor's Court. Although the exact date the force was established is unclear, in 1941, the city commission discussed constructing a new building to house both the fire department and the police force. Regardless of the date, one or both of the holding cells were eventually moved to inside the firehouse, next to where the fire truck was kept. The small square cell, estimated at about eight by eight feet in size, consisted of strips of flat metal running horizontally and vertically, riveted together, as opposed to bars. The gaps between the interlocking metal strips looked like little squares and were described as big enough for a man to put his fist through.

In December 1946, the *Safety Harbor Herald* reported that the city hired Clearwater resident Howard E. Benson to be its sole patrolman and therefore chief of police, replacing W.E. Kirk, who had resigned. Chief Benson had served with the Chicago Police Department prior to coming to the area and, at an estimated 350 pounds, was believed to be one of the largest officers in Florida at the time. One longtime resident confided that this estimate was considerably low. In what might have been an attempt at dry humor or Benson's attempt to allay doubts about his capabilities, the *Herald* reported that at his introduction to the city commission, Chief Benson portrayed himself as "of an athletic nature [capable of] swim[ming] a distance of 20 miles and [whose] great desire is to swim the English Channel." Allegedly, because of his size, he was subject to "considerable criticism" upon taking the job. Benson contended with citizens' complaints until he had had enough and abruptly quit in October 1950. One of the criticisms against Benson was that he always called on Constable Vasbinder to make arrests. As a result, all fines collected as a result of legal violations went into the county coffer and added nothing to the city treasury. "What else could I do?" asked Benson. "The city has no police court and no jail. What would I do with them if I arrest them myself?" It was also reported that if a violator refused to pay a fine, he would be transferred from the small holding cell to the county jail, and Safety Harbor would be held responsible for the costs of his keep, which the city could ill afford.

Between 1950 and 1957, at least four different men served as Safety Harbor's chief of police. For some of that period, especially during the winter tourist months, the city added a second officer, but turnover was rampant. When patrolman Glenn Gammage resigned in March 1957 after just one month on the job, he was the fifth patrolman to quit in less than a year, leaving Chief John Anderson, who had himself been recently hired, as the sole member of the city's police department. Anderson became embroiled in controversy several weeks later amid allegations that he had failed to file required reports with the city commission, leading to Mayor Downs's declaration of a citywide emergency, as detailed in Chapter 14.

Police Chief Claude Rigsby, 1958. *Photo courtesy of Safety Harbor Museum and Cultural Center.*

Anderson eventually resigned, and in April 1958, Claude Rigsby took over as Safety Harbor's new chief of police, commencing thirty years of public service to the city, including long stints as mayor and as a city commissioner.

In May 1960, after two years as chief of police, Rigsby successfully ran for constable, replacing the retiring Percy Vasbinder. Rigsby soon distinguished himself while taking part in a roadblock aimed at catching the robber of both the Oldsmar Grocery Store and the Lookout Bar in 1961. After hearing a description of the suspect, Rigsby realized that it was Gordon Abel, a man he had known since his childhood growing up in Safety Harbor. Upon seeing Abel near the Alligator Creek Dam, the unarmed Rigsby walked over and arrested him. When Abel saw Rigsby crossing the road, he reportedly said, "I'd have shot anybody but you, Claude." For this, Rigsby received an award from the National Police Officers Association the following year.

By January 1963, the city police department consisted of four full-time patrolmen and five volunteers. These volunteers, whose numbers had increased to seven by the end of the decade, had arrest powers, and each served at least sixteen hours per month. The police and the volunteer force were known to stay out of the areas where the African American community lived, but the constable handled complaints in that part of town.

There were plenty of accusations of improper behavior and scandals. In October 1971, a petition urged the abolition of the city's police department, citing "a complete breakdown of law enforcement in the city of Safety Harbor." In June 1974, a major scandal rocked the force when two patrolmen were accused of rape. The officers were dismissed, and Chief John Malamatos resigned the following day.

In early 1975, Claude Rigsby, who had become mayor in 1972, initiated the idea of abolishing the police department and contracting with the sheriff's department. Rigsby alluded to the estimated $80,000 in potential annual cost savings, although the community's shrinking confidence in the integrity of the department was undoubtedly an additional factor. Still, the following month, the city commission voted to retain the police force. Mayor Rigsby, who cast the only vote against keeping the unit, vowed that this vote would not be the end of the matter, telling the *St. Petersburg Times* that "we just can't afford [the police force]."

The following year, a citywide referendum was held, and Safety Harbor residents voted to allow abolition of the police department to be effective June 25, 1976. Since that time, Safety Harbor has been protected by the Pinellas County Sheriff's Department.

THE SAFETY HARBOR FIRE DEPARTMENT

The bucket brigades and gunshot fire alarms that made up the city's early days of firefighting changed dramatically when Safety Harbor purchased its

The Rigsby twins on one of Safety Harbor's first fire trucks. *Photo courtesy of Clyde Rigsby.*

first fire truck, a secondhand American LaFrance in July 1923. The following year, a building was erected to house the vehicle, and in July 1925, the city commission and the fire department established the city's first fire ordinances and building safety laws. Fires were common throughout the small city, as homes were made of wood, and outdoor cooking as well as cooking over fires was customary. People used their fireplaces to heat their homes in winter, and faulty fireplaces were to blame for a high percentage of blazes. Many homes were completely lost due to fires. Soon, a second fire truck was acquired, possibly erected on a Ford Model T chassis, and the city organized its first official volunteer fire department.

During Safety Harbor's financial difficulties of the post-boom years and the Great Depression, all city services except the fire department were discontinued. Because it could not afford the cost of repairs and maintenance, Safety Harbor found itself with two undependable fire trucks by the early 1930s. On December 9, 1936, a call to help was written in the *Herald* during a week in which several fires had occurred. "On at least two occasions the fire trucks have been hard to start," wrote Shower, who went on to say that the city did not have the funding to pay the town mechanic to fix them. In an editorial, he pleaded with the citizens to donate fifty cents or one dollar per month to help. The following week's paper reported that the fire department had been reorganized.

In 1941, when the city was preparing for emergencies in the months following the start of World War II, a building was selected on the south side of Main Street to house both the fire department and the police. Around the same time, the city began organizing patrols and extensively training firefighters and many citizens in first aid. Franklin Shower, who would later take his father's place as editor of the *Herald*, was appointed fire chief in November 1943.

Although there were many to help when fire struck, obstacles still sometimes hampered the department. The *Evening Independent* published details of a fire in March 1945 that destroyed a home built and originally occupied by the Pedigo family. As was reported, flames from a fire set by boys to clear brush quickly caught the wind and found the home's dry roof. The Safety Harbor Fire Department responded quickly, but "there being no water available, there was nothing they could do."

Bobby Morrow moved to Safety Harbor in the mid-1940s. His father was a mechanic and needed a garage where he could work. "The City of Safety Harbor said to my dad that he could have the stall behind the fire station as a place to work, but he had to get the fire truck to start under its own power. Up until then they had to push the fire truck to get it started."

It was common for kids to rush toward the station when the fire alarm rang out. Morrow continued, "Everyone wanted to see the fire. Most of us would follow on our bikes. It couldn't have been too far. Safety Harbor was pretty small."

By the fall of 1947, work had started on a new fire station, and a twenty-four-hour fire alarm system was desired. But there was a problem: the alarm system required a private telephone line. City hall had the only available line, so it was moved to the fire station, and city hall was connected through a party line.

Mechanical issues continued to plague the department. After the occurrence of many false alarms, a decision was made in the latter part of 1951 to operate the fire alarm system manually. The American LaFrance truck required extensive repairs at a cost that made the commissioners wonder about purchasing a new truck. About the same time, a 1941 Buick ambulance was donated to the city by Rhodes Funeral Home, but necessary repairs would prove to cost the department over $300, a bit high for its budget.

The city's Model T fire truck was sold to a fire museum for $100 in 1955. Meanwhile, a new truck was greatly needed, so the city agreed to purchase a new American LaFrance truck in December of that same year. Five years later, the city's first ladder truck was sold for $350.

Over the next several years, a fire prevention code was adopted, and a new pumper and fire protective clothing were purchased. When Hurricane Gladys struck the city in 1968, the fire department was ready to help. The firefighters cleared roadways of hazardous debris and stood watch over fallen power lines during the night. Then, in 1973, Wayne Stuart, a twenty-year veteran with the Gary, Indiana Fire Department, joined the Safety Harbor department to work as "captain in charge of supervision and training." He was the city's first paid captain.

During a time of increasing growth and new housing development, a second attempt at an ordinance to ban open fires passed unanimously in June 1979 as cheers rang out from citizens attending the city commission meeting. The *St. Petersburg Times* reported that "the ordinance was aimed primarily at developers of this boom area whose land-clearing machinery would pile stacks of felled trees that would then be set afire."

Today, the Safety Harbor Fire Department provides emergency medical services and responds to emergencies in Safety Harbor, West Oldsmar and Tampa Bay. They also provide mutual aid to other surrounding districts. There are two fire stations in Safety Harbor's city limits: Station 53 at 3095 McMullen Booth Road and Station 52 at 700 Main Street.

A Short History of Safety Harbor's Schools

As mentioned in Chapter 7, pioneer James P. "Captain Jim" McMullen built the first area school for his children and his neighbors' children in 1853 or 1854 near the current Sylvan Abbey Cemetery.

The first school in the city limits began around 1905 and was located behind where the fire station now stands on Main Street and was described as a two-room frame building for white students in grades one through eight. High school students traveled outside the city to attend Clearwater High.

In 1916, the students moved to a new three-story red brick building at 535 Fifth Avenue North. The Safety Harbor School continued there, educating elementary and middle school students to ninth grade. The Safety Harbor School expanded in 1926 with new, larger classrooms and an auditorium.

The black community was served by the Lincoln Heights School, located at 675 Elm Avenue North. The Lincoln Heights School was built in 1926, during segregation, and educated 68 black students when it first opened. In 1948, the school was consolidated and merged with Clearwater's Wilson School. In 1959, four classrooms were built on Elm Avenue, and 121 students attended the new Lincoln Heights Elementary.

By the early 1960s, Safety Harbor's population had grown, and larger facilities were required. To meet the demand for additional space, Safety Harbor Junior High opened in February 1962 at 125 Seventh Street North. At the time there were three hundred middle-grade students in attendance from Safety Harbor and neighboring communities. In 2004, a new building was constructed on the same grounds.

By 1969, schools were no longer segregated, and all of Safety Harbor's children were finally permitted to attend Safety Harbor School together. The Lincoln Heights School closed for remodeling and repairs. It reopened one

The Safety Harbor School, currently part of the expanded Safety Harbor Elementary.
Photo courtesy of Heritage Village Archives and Library.

year later as the Safety Harbor Exceptional School and provided education to students with special needs for many years.

Today, Safety Harbor serves students through public and private schools, including Safety Harbor Elementary, Safety Harbor Middle School, Espiritu Santo Catholic School, Safety Harbor Montessori Academy, North Bay Christian Academy and the Florida Sheriffs Youth Ranch. The nearest public high school is Countryside High School in Clearwater.

THE SAFETY HARBOR LIBRARY'S BEGINNINGS

The possibility of obtaining a library for the city of Safety Harbor was first mentioned in the minutes of the October 19, 1938 meeting of the Women's Civic Club, when a committee was formed to investigate the feasibility of opening a library funded through the Works Progress Administration. The WPA was one of President Roosevelt's New Deal programs, which assisted many communities, often through the provision of funding for new public buildings and roads.

Soon it was announced that funding would be provided to establish the city's first public library, to be located at the Community House on Second Street North, in the same building where the Women's Civic Club held its meetings. The Women's Civic Club was responsible for paying the transportation charges on books from Jacksonville and for returning them at regular intervals. The club was also responsible for maintaining the building.

On November 25, 1938, a woman named Daisy Cahow accepted the WPA's appointment as librarian. That month, Mrs. Cahow reported that approximately one hundred books were on the shelves, not including the volumes on loan from Jacksonville, and that gifts and loans of books would be appreciated. The *Safety Harbor Herald* advertised library hours, a children's program and requests for books. Children's Hour was scheduled for Saturday mornings. Mrs. Cahow would later be rated by the WPA as one of the top librarians in the district.

Over time, the inventory increased, often through gifts of books from members of the community. By April 1940, the facility contained 800 volumes, and before the end of the year, two large donations from a Clearwater resident and the Enoch Pratt Library in Baltimore brought the total to 1,500.

In March 1942, the WPA ended all funding for libraries in the state of Florida. After some discussion, however, the Civic Club decided to self-fund the facility, agreeing to retain Mrs. Cahow as the librarian at a salary of five dollars a week, assisted by a team of volunteers. The library was set to be open from

1:00 to 5:00 p.m., Tuesday through Friday, but within a few years, the hours of operation were drastically reduced. A number of women volunteered their time through the remainder of the war to keep the library from closing. The women organized teas to raise money.

The efforts of the Women's Civic Club paid off, and the library continued to grow. By November 1946, nearly 2,500 books were on the shelves. It was becoming evident that a larger library was needed, and discussions on how to accomplish this were ongoing. Dr. Salem Baranoff, the new owner of the Safety Harbor Resort and Spa, offered to purchase and donate land for a new building. The new building was completed in November 1949. In 1994, a new library was constructed on Second Street North, which was later expanded by an additional 60 percent of space.

In April 2013, the library celebrated its seventy-fifth anniversary. Today, the Safety Harbor Public Library is a vibrant center of learning that would certainly make its founders proud. Thousands of books, a vast music and movie collection and online resources cater to the community's thirst for knowledge and entertainment. Workshops, tutoring, deaf literacy services, poetry readings and author talks are among the programs offered. "Things have not changed that much," wrote librarian Lisa Kothe. "We held a wine and cheese Friends of the Library fundraiser with a solo performer for entertainment, and we still hold Story Times, a highly attended library staple."

Postmaster Shower's Famous Dispatch Desk

For the few settlers living in the area that would one day be named Safety Harbor, a post office was established on February 7, 1890, with Seymour Youngblood as the first postmaster. Postmaster Youngblood served for five years. Several postmasters followed, including, for a short time, Richard Booth. In 1905, mail was sorted by Postmaster George Thomas and picked up at the local grocery store, where the postmaster kept a large dispatch desk with small slots for holding letters and other mail. Often the postmaster was also a local grocer or businessperson who had other work to do during the day besides handling mail.

The dispatch desk was sold to each new postmaster who followed until it came into the possession of Dwight W. Shower. Shower, one of the sons of *Safety Harbor Herald* founder and longtime editor A.E. Shower, would remain the city's postmaster for thirty-two years, until his retirement in 1970. The desk is now on permanent loan to the Safety Harbor Museum and Cultural Center.

Chapter 16

TODAY'S SAFETY HARBOR

One hundred years ago, people traveled to Safety Harbor to drink the mineral water from Espiritu Santo Springs in search of cures. Now the Safety Harbor Resort and Spa attracts visitors from all over the world for its many amenities, even though the story of Hernando de Soto and the Fountain of Youth is considered treasured folklore by modern historians and scholars.

Written accounts demonstrate that from pioneer days onward, the people who have loved and lived in Safety Harbor developed a strong sense of community. Fish fries and church revivals of yesteryear have become today's festivals, parades, the Third Friday Music Series and other events that bring thousands of visitors annually.

Only a small percentage of the bricks that once paved early Main Street remain, but the wildlife and natural beauty of the town are a constant link that residents past and present have enjoyed. There are still people traveling around town on bicycles, and as it has always been, the pier is still considered one of the city's most enjoyable locations. Today's Safety Harbor

Most of Main Street's unique shops, restaurants and pubs are locally owned and operated. *Photo by Terrie Thomas.*

is a modern small city with a growing downtown business district, numerous parks, strong cultural and arts support, top-rated schools, community and recreation centers and fire and rescue services to make any city proud.

Festivals, Fundraisers and Third Fridays

Those who visit Safety Harbor often comment on the fun, family-friendly way in which the residents, businesses and city encourage playfulness. Back in Safety Harbor's early years, townspeople gathered for parades, carnivals and festivals that often celebrated the rich history of Florida and its people.

Festivals like the British Car Show attract thousands of visitors to Safety Harbor each year. *Photo by Marcia Biggs.*

They paved the way for coming generations to celebrate life in the Tampa Bay area's most beautiful city.

Not only have the festivals become annual celebrations, but there is also an event that brings thousands to the city every third Friday of each month. Once a month from January through December, Main Street is closed to automobile traffic. Businesses stay open late, vendors line both sides of the street and live music mixes with the sounds of neighbors, friends and strangers enjoying an evening out. A featured musician or band performs in the gazebo in John Wilson Park. Dogs are welcome, prices are affordable and many businesses offer special food and beverage choices.

PARKS AND RECREATION

Safety Harbor's Community Center is located at 650 Ninth Avenue South. The Rigsby Recreation Center, named for Claude Rigsby, is downtown at 605 Second Street North. Both offer opportunities such as camps, after-school programs, sports and learning support. The Safety Harbor Museum and Cultural Center at 329 Bayshore Boulevard also promotes education through lectures and traveling exhibits and hosts many summer camps for children and teens.

The Museum and Cultural Center offers a view into Safety Harbor's past through numerous artifacts and photographs. It is run by a board of directors and staffed by a curator and volunteers. In addition, a group of citizens has formed a historical society to help preserve the city's history.

The Safety Harbor Garden Club consistently beautifies and cares for many of the city's public spaces, as evidenced by Mullet Creek Park, one of the newest of the city's dozen parks. The city park system offers a wide range of recreation opportunities in a variety of settings.

Men and women who have served in the U.S. military are remembered at the Veterans Memorial Park, adjacent to the marina, where manatees and dolphins often can be seen playing in the water around the fishing pier. A kayak launch and a boat ramp allow access to upper Tampa Bay. The green land abutting the shoreline to the left of the marina (unnamed as of this writing) is the newest Safety Harbor park, a place to picnic, throw a Frisbee or walk along the bay. Plans are in place to add a small beach, a water park for children and nature trails through the wooded area to the north.

Manatees swim near the marina and pier. *Photo by Terrie Thomas.*

The Bayshore Linear Greenway Recreational Trail provides a measured recreational path for runners, walkers, bicyclists and skaters. The trail begins at the fountain near the marina on South Bayshore Boulevard. Not far away, on Main Street, John Wilson Park's gazebo is the place to take part in the farmers' market, the annual holiday tree lighting and Third Friday concerts.

Children play at Marshall Street Park and Daisy Douglas Park, the latter of which is named for a powerful leader who for many years helped to bridge race relations and better the community as a whole. In addition, a little farther from the town center are two other play areas, North City Park, which is tucked into the neighborhoods of Harbor Woods and North Bay Hills, and Mease Park. Safety Harbor City Park covers twenty-one acres and offers a fenced dog park, playgrounds and a public boat ramp to Alligator Lake. There are also baseball fields and picnic areas. The skate park there is named in memory of Ian Tilmann, who died from brain injuries incurred from a skateboarding accident when not wearing a helmet. His death inspired the Helmet for a Promise program, which started at the skate park in 2006. Since that time, 1,400 free helmets have been given to skaters at the skate park. Ian's parents, Marcy and Barry Tilmann, have been residents of Safety Harbor for over twenty-five years.

Spanish moss hangs from reaching oaks in Philippe Park. *Photo by Terrie Thomas.*

Two small parks are located on land adjacent to the public library. One of these, the Art Park, is located on the land that once contained the Pipkin shell mound. Now, visitors can relax among benches and a picnic table while shaded by old oak trees draped with Spanish moss. The second, Baranoff Park, features the large oak in front of the library. This tree was officially named the Baranoff Oak in 2004 after the former spa owner whose generous donation of land allowed the library to grow from its humble beginnings. Immediately thereafter, the tree was added to a national registry of oak trees maintained by the Live Oak Society of the Louisiana Garden Club Federation.

Perhaps the most acclaimed is Philippe Park, the oldest in the county. The park is set along a one-mile shoreline of Old Tampa Bay. It is named for Odet Philippe and is the location that was once most of the original Philippe plantation. Safety Harbor's one remaining Tocobaga Indian mound stands high in the middle of the park and is listed as a National Historic Landmark. The mound can be climbed by stairway or walkway. Visitors may enjoy picnicking, fishing, playgrounds, a rock climbing park, a ball field and open spaces. Joggers and cyclists utilize the main road, shaded by a gauntlet of moss-draped southern oaks. A public boat ramp is available during park hours.

What Remains: Original Buildings and Points of Interest

A number of buildings and structures from the early days of the city's history, including several that have been mentioned previously, still stand and continue to be utilized today.

Built in 1915, the small building at 200 Main Street survived the 1917 fire that destroyed surrounding structures. Over the years, it was home to the town's first bank and, later, city hall. The building is now occupied by the Safety Harbor Chamber of Commerce.

With three levels, the original St. James Hotel, at 101 Main Street, has been converted to the Safety Harbor Senior Living facility. The assisted living center's office faces the beautiful Baranoff Oak tree. A variety of retail shops and businesses, including the flower shop operated by B.J. Lehman, line the south and west sides of the building.

For many years, the original St. Frances Hotel at 454 Main Street was declared haunted, but before her death, Mrs. Bertha (McElveen) Rountree, whose family operated the hotel during the early part of the twentieth century, dispelled these rumors. Today, the lower level hosts a retail store, while the building's upper level is divided into apartments, including one occupied by Caryl Dennis, who offers psychic readings from this location and has had her own "experiences" there. "I'm not so sure it isn't haunted," she said.

Almost one hundred years ago, the first *Tropical Breeze* and later the *Safety Harbor Herald* operated out of a building located in today's John Wilson Park. After the paper expanded, it moved to 525 Main Street, which is currently a retail store.

The first dedicated library is now utilized by Harborside Studios, which is an arts studio and gallery catering to artists with special needs.

Outside the northwest corner of the current library is a water pump once located on the property of the home of D.M. Pipkin. A historical marker nearby explains that this pump was used by local residents to access drinking water from one of the area's five mineral springs.

Other structures with interesting histories include the mansion built by Virginia Tucker, which stands at 311 North Bayshore Drive, and an old capped well that is situated on the property of the Safety Harbor Museum and Cultural Center. Many other buildings in or around the downtown area have equally fascinating ties to the city's past.

The Arts: Safety Harbor's True Link
to the Fountain of Youth

About thirty years ago, Todd Ramquist and Kiaralinda began transforming their gray home with bright, eye-popping colors, decorating their yard with art and surrounding it with one-of-a-kind painted bowling balls. This house (called the Whimzey House) is a popular tourist attraction, and the artists welcome visitors on the property at 1206 Third Street North. Todd and Kiaralinda are now the moving forces behind much of the city's art events and culture. Their home has been featured on television programs such as *60 Minutes*, *Oprah*, MTV's *Extreme Cribs* and HGTV. In 2010, they received a $50,000 Pepsi Refresh Grant to build a center for the arts. Since then they have raised more funds to complete the Safety Harbor Art and Music Center at 706 Second Street North.

The Syd Entel Galleries and Susan Benjamin Glass have been on Main Street for thirty-two years, twenty-two of which have been at their current location. The five-thousand-square-foot combined gallery showcases fine art and glass art by nationally and internationally acclaimed artists.

Safety Harbor is a haven for musicians and music lovers. There are jazz, blues, rock, reggae, country and many other live music genres played at arts and crafts and other festivals throughout the year and also along Main Street

The eclectic Whimzey House at 1206 Third Street North. *Photo by Holly Apperson.*

on numerous evenings per month. Musicians also have the benefit of joining the Tampa Bay Musicians' Co-op, located just off Main and Seventh Streets.

Perhaps because the city is so art-friendly, a small group of volunteers has succeeded in growing an annual Chalk Festival. Every spring, Main Street's sidewalks are decorated with scenes depicting sea life, nature, history and more. This event reminds residents of the quaint yet powerfully creative charm that pervades the city.

Watercolor painting, drawing, cartooning, creative writing, photography and bead-making classes are some of the many classes available through the Safety Harbor Museum and Cultural Center.

The City of Safety Harbor Public Art Committee is a strong, supportive committee dedicated to publicly showcasing local artists' works. The city actively seeks artists to display their works at the library and at city hall throughout the year.

The Players of Safety Harbor (P.O.S.H.) is a community theater group established in 2004. Performances are held at the Safety Harbor Library. Its goal is to "provide opportunities for people of all ages to develop their talents and skills through drama and entertainment."

The Safety Harbor Library attracts writers and poets from surrounding cities due to its wide array of classes, workshops and lectures pertaining to literary arts. Every spring, the library hosts a Poetry Festival. It is no wonder Safety Harbor has been home to many musicians, visual artists, poets, writers and sculptors.

The Safety Harbor Marina. *Photo by Warren Firschein.*

Whether Hernando de Soto actually landed on the shores of Safety Harbor may never be known, but Safety Harbor has every right to claim that it is a true "Health Giving City," if not from its natural springs, then at least from the sunshine, friendliness and the general spirit of community that binds generations of Safety Harbor's residents and the city's friends and supporters.

Early pioneers worked hard and probably had little time for leisure as they raised children, harvested food and faced nature's harsh discomforts. But perhaps there were moments when those who came before us thought of future generations and wondered what their city on the bay would look like...someday.

MAYORS OF THE CITY OF
SAFETY HARBOR

G.W. Campbell, 1917–19

C.S. Washington, 1919–21

C.A. Boynton, 1921–22

D.M. Pipkin, 1922–23, 1924

W.L. Hackney, 1923–24, 1924–25

J. Daniel Bozardt, 1925–26

George Booth, 1926–27

W.E. Edwards, 1927–29

L.H. Zinsser, 1929–42, 1944–46

George Sward, 1942–44

Eldon Deuel, 1946–47

J.P. Melser, 1947–50

Con Barth, 1950–52

Paul McElveen, 1952–56

Ben L. Downs, 1956–60, 1962–64

Sam Douglas, 1960

Howard Martin, 1960–62

Appendix 1

George McGonegal, 1964–71

Robert Balch, 1971–72

Claude Rigsby, 1972–77, 1979–81

Charles Styron, 1977–79

Doris Jean Mellema, 1981–82

John Williams, 1982–84

Alton R. Dettmer, 1984–89

Arthur Levine, 1989–93

Kent Runnells, 1993–1996

Patrick Slevin, 1996–99

Pam Corbino, 1999–2006

Andy Steingold, 2006–13

Joseph Ayoub, 2013–present

LIST OF POSTMASTERS OF THE CITY
OF SAFETY HARBOR

NAME	TITLE	DATE APPOINTED
Seymour S. Youngblood	Postmaster	2/7/1890
Richard J. Booth	Postmaster	9/7/1895
Annell A. Blanton	Postmaster	10/23/1895
James J. Youngblood	Postmaster	5/5/1897
Seymour S. Youngblood	Postmaster	6/28/1901
John C. Heard	Postmaster	11/16/1903
Edward R. Washington	Postmaster	6/7/1904
George B. Thomas	Postmaster	7/3/1905
Emma D. Thomas	Postmaster	3/25/1914
Michael Poppler	Postmaster	1/27/1923
George B. Thomas Jr.	Postmaster	5/10/1923
Abraham H. Lasher	Acting Postmaster	5/1/1925
Abraham H. Lasher	Postmaster	12/18/1925
James A. Brown	Acting Postmaster	10/01/1934
James A. Brown	Postmaster	1/17/1935
Dwight W. Shower	Acting Postmaster	4/5/1937
Dwight W. Shower	Postmaster	6/23/1938
Mrs. Lillian R. Blanchard	Officer-in-Charge	7/24/1970
Gerald H. Ohmstede	Officer-in-Charge	2/25/1972

Mrs. Lillian R. Blanchard	Officer-in-Charge	6/29/1972
Arthur P. Burgess Jr.	Officer-in-Charge	1/19/1973
Arthur P. Burgess Jr.	Postmaster	8/25/1973
Duane L. Allen	Officer-in-Charge	5/20/1988
George R. Hammond	Officer-in-Charge	7/22/1988
Antonios E. Koutsourais	Postmaster	1/28/1989
Joe Tippanelli	Officer-in-Charge	4/7/1992
Vance David Fairbanks	Postmaster	1/9/1993
Gerald G. Peruzzi	Officer-in-Charge	6/6/1997
Rae M. DiCapua	Postmaster	8/2/1997
Sherry L. Ulrich	Officer-in-Charge	2/19/1999
Thomas H. Testa Jr.	Postmaster	5/8/1999
Brian R. Strasser	Officer-in-Charge	2/5/2002
Russell D. Miller	Postmaster	1/11/2003
Brian R. Strasser	Officer-in-Charge	5/31/2003
Christopher B. Terhune	Postmaster	8/9/2003
Brian R. Strasser	Officer-in-Charge	12/13/2004
Robert L. Ulrich	Officer-in-Charge	6/23/2005
Robert L. Ulrich	Postmaster	10/1/2005
Brian R. Strasser	Officer-in-Charge	5/27/2006
Brian R. Strasser	Postmaster	8/5/2006

APPROXIMATE ANNUAL FESTIVAL SCHEDULE

The following is a list of special events that were scheduled to occur in Safety Harbor in 2013 and are reasonably expected to continue on an ongoing basis. Approximate dates are provided to assist with future years' planning. This list does not include races, such as the St. Patrick's Day 5K Run sponsored by Nolan's Pub and the Jingle Bell Run in mid-December, which are periodically planned through the streets of the city.

MONTH	APPROXIMATE DATE	EVENT
January–December	Third Friday of each month	Street/Music Festival
June–September	One Saturday mid-month	Summer Farmers' Market Open
October–May	Each Thursday	Farmers' Market Open
January	Mid-month	Senior Expo
February	Saturday before February 14	Daddy Daughter Date Night
	Last weekend	San Gennaro Italian Festival

March	Weekend, early March	Seafood Festival
	Weekend, late March	Chalk Art Festival
April	Saturday, early April	Truck-N-Play Day
July	July 4	July 4 Parade and Celebration
August	Saturday, mid-August	Back to School Bash
October	Weekend, early October	Harbor Sounds Music Festival
	Saturday, late October	All British Car Show
	October 31	Main Street Trick-or-Treat
November	Saturday, early November	Wine Festival
December	Friday, early December	Tree Lighting
	Saturday, early December	Snowfest
	Sunday, early December	Kiwanis Arts & Crafts Show
	Saturday before Christmas	Holiday Parade

BIBLIOGRAPHY

Abbott, John S.C. *Fernando De Soto, the Discoverer of the Mississippi.* New York: Dodd & Mead, 1873.

Anonymous. *Espiritu Santo Springs, On Old Tampa Bay, near Tampa, Fla.* Green Springs, FL: Espiritu Santo Springs, 1910.

———. "History of the Safety Harbor Library." Date unknown. Shelved at the Safety Harbor Public Library.

Archaeological Consultants, Inc. *Archaeological Assessment Survey, Morton Plant Mease Countryside Hospital— North Campus Improvements, Pinellas County, Florida.* Performed for Lloveras, Baur and Stevens, Clearwater, FL. Sarasota, FL: Archaeological Consultants, Inc., 1999.

Arnade, Charles W. "The Tampa Bay Area From the Aborigines to the Spanish." *Tampa Bay History* 1, no. 1 (1979): 5–16.

Arries, D.E. "Personal Letter to City of Safety Harbor." August 30, 1935.

Austin, Robert J., Howard F. Hansen and Charles Fuhrmeister. *An Archaeological and Historical Survey of the Unincorporated Areas of Pinellas County, Florida.* Conducted for the Pinellas County Board of County Commissioners, Clearwater, FL. St. Petersburg, FL: Piper Archaeological Research, Inc., 1991.

Authentic Artifact Collectors Association. "Safety Harbor." http://www.theaaca.com/typology/safetyharbor.html (accessed July 19, 2013).

Bash, Evelyn C. "Profiles of Early Settlers on the Pinellas Peninsula." *Tampa Bay History* 5, no. 1 (1983): 82–93.

Bethel, John A. *Bethel's History of Point Pinellas.* St. Petersburg, FL: Great Outdoors Publishing Co., 1962. [Originally published as John A. Bethel, *History of Pinellas Peninsula.* St. Petersburg, FL: Press of the Independent Job Department, 1914.]

Blakesley, Elsie. "Safety Harbor Calls in County Patrol." *St. Petersburg Times,* April 16, 1957.

Booth, Mrs. George W. "Romantic Story of Dr. Philippe, Safety Harbor's First Settler." *Tampa Sunday Tribune,* May 1, 1921.

BoxingVideoFightFinder.com. Other Content DVD Database. http://www.boxingvideofightfinder.com/othercontentview.php?ID=292 (accessed August 17, 2013).

Boyd, Mark F. "The Arrival of De Soto's Expedition in Florida." *Florida Historical Quarterly* 16, no. 3 (January 1938): 188–220.

Brain, Jeffrey P. "Introduction: Update of De Soto Studies since the United States De Soto Expedition Commission Report." In John R. Swanton, *Final Report of the United States De Soto Expedition Commission,* pp. xi-lxxii. Reprint of the 1939 edition with an introduction by Jeffrey P. Brain. Washington, D.C.: Smithsonian Institution Press, 1985.

Brown, Lana. "The Safety Harbor Spa." Presented to Mr. Garrett, State and Local Government, April 15, 1966.

Brush, Frances. "Negro Wins City Election." *St. Petersburg Times,* November 11, 1964.

Bullen, Ripley P. "Archeology of the Tampa Bay Area," *Florida Historical Quarterly* 34, no. 1 (July 1955): 51–63.

———. "De Soto's Ucita and the Terra Ceia Site," *Florida Historical Quarterly* 30, no. 4 (April 1952): 317–23.

———. "Tocobaga Indians and the Safety Harbor Culture." In *Tacachale: Essays on the Indians of Florida and Southeastern Georgia during the Historic Period,* edited by Jerald T. Milanich and Samuel Proctor, pp. 50–57. Gainesville: University Presses of Florida, 1978.

Burnett, Gene M. *Florida's Past: People & Events that Shaped the State.* Vol. 1. Sarasota, FL: Pineapple Press, 1986.

———. *Florida's Past: People & Events that Shaped the State.* Vol. 2. Sarasota, FL: Pineapple Press, 1988.

———. *Florida's Past: People & Events that Shaped the State.* Vol. 3. Sarasota, FL: Pineapple Press, 1991.

Campbell, Elizabeth Snedecor. "Written During a Visit to Safety Harbor, February 1926." In Emily Boland. "The Family Book." Unpublished ms., 1965.

Catholic Encyclopedia, s.v. "Hernando De Soto." http://www.newadvent.org/cathen/04753a.htm (accessed March 10, 2013).

Clayton, Lawrence A., Vernon James Knight Jr. and Edward C. Moore, eds. *The De Soto Chronicles: The Expedition of Hernando De Soto to North America in 1539–1543.* Vol. 1. Tuscaloosa: University of Alabama Press, 1993.

Costrini-Perez, Patricia. *A Tradition of Excellence, Pinellas County Schools: 1912–1987.* Clearwater: School Board of Pinellas County, Florida, 1987.

Davis, David Brion. "Impact of the French and Haitian Revolutions." In *The Impact of the Haitian Revolution in the Atlantic World*, edited by David P. Geggus. Columbia: University of South Carolina Press, 2001.

Davis, Paul A. "Smithsonian Excavators Find Proof of Spanish Exploration in Pinellas Indian Burial Mound." *Evening Independent*, March 15, 1930.

DeFoor, J. Allison, II. *Odet Philippe, Peninsular Pioneer*. Safety Harbor, FL: Safety Harbor Museum of Regional History, 1997.

———. "Odet Philippe: From Charleston to Tampa Bay." *Tampa Bay History* 12, no. 2 (Fall/Winter 1990): 20–30.

Deley, Susan. "Safety Harbor Votes to Keep Police Force." *St. Petersburg Times*, July 9, 1975.

Douglas, Marjory Stoneman. *The Everglades: River of Grass*. New York: Rinehart & Co., 1947.

Downs, Katherine. "My Memories of Teaching School." Unpublished memoir, 1984.

Evening Independent. "Air-Conditioned Train is Latest." December 2, 1933.

———. "Booth Resigns as City Manager of Safety Harbor." June 24, 1944.

———. "Expecting Optional Route Plan to Draw More Travel." August 29, 1927.

———. "Police Chief Worn Out with Bickering, Quits." October 16, 1950.

———. "Safety Harbor Opens Another Big Hostelry." December 16, 1929.

———. "Safety Harbor Revives Old Days in May Day Festival Tomorrow." May 11, 1927.

———. "Safety Harbor Spa's Springs Dated from De Soto—State's Oldest Landmark." October 17, 1973.

———. "Sarazen Coming for Annual Open Meet Next Week." February 16, 1937.

———. "Seaboard to Operate Five Trains into City Daily During Winter." October 28, 1930.

———. "Seaboard to Put on 7 Trains." November 27, 1928.

———. "Seven of 16 Florida Casualties Last Week Not Caused by Autos." March 3, 1926.

———. "$10,000 Residence at Safety Harbor Destroyed by Fire." March 24, 1945.

———. "Town So Peaceful Nobody is Seeking Enforcement Jobs." May 9, 1936.

Firschein, Warren. Telephone interview with Bobby Morrow. Safety Harbor, July 29, 2013.

Fleischer, Mike. "A Miracle in Brooklyn—Water from the Faucet." *St. Petersburg Times*, May 12, 1969.

Florida Citrus Hall of Fame. "Odet Phillipe [*sic*] (1780–1869)." http://floridacitrushalloffame.com/index.php/inductees/inductee-name/?ref_cID=89&bID=0&dd_asId=597 (accessed June 2, 2013).

Florida Master Site File. *CRAS of the Florida Gas Transmission Company (FGT) 12-Inch St. Petersburg Relay Project, Survey No. 13051*. Florida Division of Historical Resources, Florida Department of State, Tallahassee, Florida, 2006.

———. *Cultural Resource Assessment Survey of a Portion of SR 590 from Joyce Street to Enterprise Road, Pinellas County, Florida, Survey No. 4540*. Florida Division of Historical Resources, Florida Department of State, Tallahassee, Florida, 1995.

———. *Cultural Resource Assessment of the 19.5 Acre Parcel at Fairview Street and Phillippe* [sic] *Parkway, Pinellas County, Florida, Survey No. 5023*. Florida Division of Historical Resources, Florida Department of State, Tallahassee, Florida, 1997.

———. *Espiritu Santo Springs, 8PI116*. Florida Division of Historical Resources, Florida Department of State, Tallahassee, Florida, 1970.

———. *Historic Building Survey of Safety Harbor, Florida, Survey No. 3872*. Florida Division of Historical Resources, Florida Department of State, Tallahassee, Florida, 1994.

———. *Lover's Oak Shell Mound, 8PI9620*. Florida Division of Historical Resources, Florida Department of State, Tallahassee, Florida, 1996.

———. *Morton Plant Mease Hospital, Phase I, Survey No. 5802*. Florida Division of Historical Resources, Florida Department of State, Tallahassee, Florida, 1999.

———. *Report on 1989 Investigation of the Bayshore Hotel Site, Safety Harbor, Florida, Survey No. 6498*. Florida Division of Historical Resources, Florida Department of State, Tallahassee, Florida, 2002.

———. *Safety Harbor Museum Site, 8PI1693*. Florida Division of Historical Resources, Florida Department of State, Tallahassee, Florida, 1996.

———. *Safety Harbor Site, 8PI00002*. Florida Division of Historical Resources, Florida Department of State, Tallahassee, Florida, 2002.

Francis, Michael J. "The Fountain of Youth Myth." Teachingflorida.org. http://teachingflorida.org/article/fountain-of-youth-myth (accessed July 18, 2013).

Ganley, Gladys. "Way Back." Unpublished memoirs, 1966.

Gannon, Michael V. *The Cross in the Sand: The Early Catholic Church in Florida, 1513–1870*. Gainesville: University of Florida Press, 1965.

Gentleman of Elvas. "The Expedition of Hernando De Soto in southeastern North America, 1539–1543, as recounted by a member of the expedition," as abridged on http://nationalhumanitiescenter.org (accessed March 10, 2013, http://nationalhumanitiescenter.org/pds/amerbegin/exploration/text1/desoto.pdf).

George, Paul S., ed. *A Guide to the History of Florida*. New York: Greenwood Press, 1989.

Gmitter, Frederick G., Jr. "Origin, Evolution, and Breeding of the Grapefruit." In *Plant Breeding Reviews*, vol. 13, edited by Jules Janick. New York: John Wiley & Sons, 1995.

Goggin, John M. "Space and Time Perspective in Northern St. Johns Archeology, Florida." *Yale University Publications in Anthropology* 47. New Haven, CT: Yale University Press, 1952.

Goldstein, Alan. "Trainer Dismisses Leonard-Hearns Talk: A Third Fight Has Not Been Talked About." *Baltimore Sun*, January 1, 1991.

Graham, Anne. "Salem Baranoff, Safety Harbor Spa Founder." *St. Petersburg Times*, July 27, 1977.

Griffin, John W., and Ripley P. Bullen. "The Safety Harbor Site, Pinellas County, Florida." *Florida Anthropological Society Publications* 2. Gainesville: University of Florida, 1950.

Hammond, C.A. "Dr. Stroebel Reports on Southeast Florida, 1836." *Tequesta* 21 (1961): 65–75.

Hann, John H. *Indians of Central and South Florida, 1513–1763*. Gainesville: University Press of Florida, 2003.

Hawes, Leland. "Philippe: Man of Mythical Proportions." *Tampa Tribune*, June 14, 1986.

Historic Property Associates, Inc. *Historic Building Survey of Safety Harbor, Florida.* Submitted to the Safety Harbor Planning Department. St. Augustine, FL: Historic Property Associates, Inc., 1994.

Hodges, Alan W., et al. "County Property Values and Tax Impacts of Florida's Citrus Industry." University of Florida IFAS Extension, Publication #FE437. Available online at http://www.edis.ifas.ufl.edu/fe437.

Hunter, Maxwell. "Dr. Odet Philippe Was Pinellas Peninsula's First White Settler." *St. Petersburg Times*, December 20, 1936.

Inventory of Industrial Advantages, Safety Harbor, Florida. Prepared by Florida Power Corporation and Florida State Advertising Commission. 1947.

Jahoda, Gloria. *River of the Golden Ibis*. Gainesville: University Press of Florida, 1973.

Janus Research. *CRAS of the Florida Gas Transmission Company (FGT) 12-Inch St. Petersburg Relay Project Area, Pinellas County.* Prepared for Florida Gas Transmission Company, Houston, Texas. Tampa, FL: Janus Research, 2006.

———. *Cultural Resource Assessment of the 19.5 Acre Parcel at Fairview Street and Phillippe* [sic] *Parkway, Pinellas County, Florida.* Conducted for Paul H. Corace, c/o American Landmark Homes, Clearwater, Florida. St. Petersburg, FL: Janus Research, 1997.

Jarvis, Eric. "'Secrecy Has No Excuse': The Florida Land Boom, Tourism, and the 1926 Smallpox Epidemic in Tampa and Miami." *Florida Historical Quarterly* 89, no. 3 (Winter 2011): 320–46.

Kapler, Robert. "Indians Ready to Sign First Treaty since 1567." *Clearwater Sun*, December 1, 1981.

———. "Museum-Indian Treaty Set for Saturday Signing." *Clearwater Sun*, December 3, 1981.

Kaylor, Steve. "Preserving History: Safety Harbor Museum Links Youth with the Past." *Evening Independent*, July 25, 1980.

Kepner, Laura. Interview with Goldie Banks. Safety Harbor, May 30, 2013.

———. Interview with Jean Barraclough. Safety Harbor, June 3, 2013.

———. Interview with Sandie Brasfield and Dolly Brader Whitehead. Holliday, Florida, May 25, 2013.

———. Interview with Laura Dent. Safety Harbor, May 3, 2013.

———. Interview with Susanne Devnani. Safety Harbor, June 17, 2013.

———. Interview with Kim Lashington and Yvonne Hedgeman. Safety Harbor, June 3, 2013.

———. Interview with B.J. Lehman. Safety Harbor, May 30, 2013.

———. Interview with Jewel McKeon. Safety Harbor, April 22, 2013.

———. Interview with Loella Myrick. Safety Harbor, August 2, 2013.

———. Interview with Lois Spencer. Safety Harbor, May 21, 2013.

———. Interview with members of the Safety Harbor Presbyterian Church. Safety Harbor, June 23, 2013.

Kepner, Laura, and Warren Firschein. Interview with Robert Scott Anderson. Safety Harbor, March 26, 2013.

———. Interview with William Blackshear. Dunellon, July 3, 2013.

———. Interview with David Nichols. Safety Harbor, June 8, 2013.

———. Interview with Clyde Rigsby. Safety Harbor, June 21, 2013.

Klinkenberg, Jeff. "Seeded Bliss." *Tampa Bay Times*, January 29, 2005.

Koren, Herman. *Histories of the Jewish People of Pinellas County, Florida, 1883–2005, Hebrew Dates 5643–5766*. Clearwater, FL: Temple B'Nai Israel, 2007.

Lakeland Ledger. "Old Polk Album." February 8, 1985.

Lanier, Sidney. *Florida: Its Scenery, Climate and History*. Gainesville: University of Florida Press, 1973, orig. ed. 1875.

Letter from Seth S. Walker, Thornton & Co., to Dr. Con F. Barth, Safety Harbor, December 23, 1936.

Lewis, Clifford M. "The Calusa." In *Tacachale: Essays on the Indians of Florida and Southeastern Georgia during the Historic Period*, edited by Jerald T. Milanich and Samuel Proctor, pp. 27–29. Gainesville: University Press of Florida, 1978.

Lindberg, Anne. "Last Orange Grove Fades from Pinellas." *St. Petersburg Times*, September 30, 2005.

Lowery, Woodbury. *The Spanish Settlements within the Present Limits of the United States: Florida 1562–1574*. New York: Russell & Russell, 1959.

Lyon, Eugene. *The Enterprise of Florida, Pedro Menéndez de Avilés and the Spanish Conquest of 1565–1568*. Tallahassee, FL: Rose Printing Co., 1974.

Martin, Mildred. "A Tribute to Mrs. Louise A. Pearce." *Safety Harbor Herald*, November 6, 1942.

McKay, D.B. "Book Tells How De Soto's Advance Scouts Landed on Old Tampa Bay." *Tampa Tribune*, August 10, 1947.

———. "Colorful Count Planted First Citrus Grove in This Area." *Tampa Tribune*, December 29, 1946.

———. "Pioneer Florida." *Tampa Tribune*, May 17, 1959.

———. *Pioneer Florida*. Tampa, FL: Southern Publishing Company, 1959.

———. *Pioneer Florida*. Book II. Tampa, FL: Southern Publishing Company, 1959.

McKey, Mary. "Safety Harbor Police Chief Resigns." *St. Petersburg Times*, June 8, 1974.

McMullen, Ward. "Radio Interview." Undated. On file at Heritage Village, Largo, FL.

McNally, Michael J. *Catholic Parish Life on Florida's West Coast*. St. Petersburg, FL: Catholic Media Ministries, 1996.

Milanich, Jerald T. *Florida Indians and the Invasion from Europe*. Gainesville: University Press of Florida, 1995.

———. "Hernando De Soto and the Expedition in Florida: An Overview." *Florida Anthropologist* 42, no. 4 (December 1989): 303–16.

———. "Where Did de Soto Land?: Identifying Bahia Honda." *Florida Anthropologist* 42, no. 4 (December 1989): 295–302.

Milanich, Jerald T., and Charles Hudson. *Hernando de Soto and the Indians of Florida*. Gainesville: University Press of Florida, 1993.

Mitchem, Jeffrey M. "An Analysis of Artifacts from the Safety Harbor Site (8PI2), Pinellas County, Florida." *Florida Anthropologist* 47, no. 2 (June 1994): 147–60.

———. "Redefining Safety Harbor: Late Prehistoric/Protohistoric Archaeology in West Peninsular Florida." PhD diss., University of Florida, 1989.

Morison, Samuel Eliot. *The European Discovery of America: the Southern Voyages, 1492–1616*. New York: Oxford University Press, 1974.

Nabokov, Peter. *Native American Architecture*. New York: Oxford University Press, 1989.

Norwood, Olin. "Letters from Florida in 1881." *Florida Historical Quarterly* 29 (April 1951): 273–74.

Olds, Arthur F. *It's No Bull, the True Story of the Taming of Northeast Pinellas County*. New Port Richey, FL: Boot Ranch Publishing Co., 1992.

Pavluvcik, Tom. *Trains of Pinellas County*. Vol. 1, *The Early Years, St. Petersburg–Clearwater Railroad History in Pictures*. N.p.: self-published, 2013. Available online at www.tampabaytrains.com.

Pinellas Times. "Safety Harbor Candidates Stress Tighter Purse Strings." February 1, 1976.

Pochurek, Patricia. *Remembering Safety Harbor*. Safety Harbor, FL: Tropical Breeze Publications, 1992.

Reed, Ralph. "Pinellas Citrus Groves Periled as Bottom Falls Out of Market." *St. Petersburg Times*, March 12, 1948.

Reilly, Stephen Edward. "A Marriage of Expedience: The Calusa Indians and Their Relations with Pedro Menéndez de Avilés in Southwest Florida, 1566–1569." *Florida Historical Quarterly* 59, no. 4 (April 1981): 395–421.

Reinhartz, Dennis, and Oakah L. Jones. "Hacia el Norte! The Spanish Entrada into North America, 1513–1549." In *North American Exploration*, Vol. 1, *A New World Disclosed*, edited by John Logan Allen, pp. 241–291. Lincoln: University of Nebraska Press, 1997.

Robinson, T. Ralph. "Count Odet Philippe—A Correction to Florida's Citrus Past." *Florida State Horticultural Society Journal* (1947): 90–92.

Rosenfield, Jeffrey. "Who Will Save the Safety Harbor Black Cemetery?" *Safety Harbor Patch*, posted July 1, 2013. http://safetyharbor.patch.com/groups/editors-picks/p/who-will-save-the-safety-harbor-black-cemetery (accessed August 21, 2013).

Safety Harbor Area Historical Society. "Activities Report, 1967–68."

———. "Remember When," *Tocobaga Newsletter* 10, no. 5 (May 1977).

Safety Harbor Herald. Uncaptioned news item, February 7, 1919.

———. Uncaptioned news item, November 21, 1919.

———. "A.E. Shower Passed Away Tuesday, January 31." February 2, 1961.

———. "Ben L. Downs Retained as Mayor by 230 to 164 Votes of Citizens in Monday's Recall Election." September 13, 1957.

———. "Big Street Carnival to be Held Tomorrow Night—Plenty of Fun for All." January 5, 1941.

———. "Bill to Reduce City Limits Becomes Law." June 16, 1933.

———. "Citrus Patent is Given Safety Harbor Inventor." February 26, 1937.

———. "City Commissioners Prepare for Action under Wilcox Act." August 20, 1937.

———. "City to Experience First Test Blackout Tonight." January 2, 1942.

———. "Colored School Children Purchase Savings Stamps." October 24, 1941.

———. "Colored Singers from Tampa to Entertain Sunday." July 16, 1937.

———. "Curb Coming for the Street Paving Work." March 19, 1926.

———. "Dwelling Destroyed in Early Morning Blaze." August 20, 1937.

———. "Espiritu Santo Springs Fountain Water Free to Public." January 7, 1927.

———. "Facts about the City of Safety Harbor." June 10, 1932.

———. "Fire Department is Re-Organized." December 16, 1932.

———. "Fire Destroys Two Seminole Park Residences Thursday AM." December 9, 1932.

———. "Fire in One of the Cassarow Cottages." February 12, 1926.

———. "Girl Diamond Ball Team Swamp Clearwater Girls." June 21, 1935.

———. "Horse Racing Resumed at Sunshine Park." January 24, 1947.

———. "Jail Cells Arrive for City Lock-Up." February 19, 1926.

———. "Kirk Resigns – Benson Employed Chief of Police." December 13, 1946.

———. "Lawton Harrington Legion Post Formed." July 28, 1944.

———. "Letter to the Editor." January 8, 1926.

———. "Letter to the Editor." January 29, 1960.

———. "Money Needed to Complete Fire Station." November 14, 1947.

———. "More Cases of Small Pox in Colored Quarters." January 15, 1926.

———. "Mrs. Mary Ingersoll New City Manager." June 23, 1944.

———. "New Fire Truck Pays for Itself in Two Fires This Week." January 14, 1927.

———. "No New Cases of Smallpox Develop." January 22, 1926.

———. "1,435 Skeletons Unearthed in Indian Burial Mound." April 4, 1930.

———. "O.W. Booth Sr. Has Narrow Escape from Serious Injury." November 22, 1929.

———. "Packing House Ready for Work." November 21, 1919.

———. "Paper Keeping Up With City." February 5, 1926.

———. "Police Chief Claude Rigsby Announces Candidacy for Constable 3 Post." July 27, 1962.

———. "Rainbow Feast." May 13, 1921.

———. "Safety Harbor Seeks D'Soto Landing Marker." December 18, 1936.

———. "Safety Harbor's Proposed Freshwater Lake from the Air" December 26, 1947.

———. "Safety Harbor Votes to Reduce City Limits." July 21, 1933.

———. "Santo Springs Water Now Free to Visitors at Remodeled Spa." December 18, 1936.

———. "Seaboard Train Kills Mrs. Louise A. Pearce." November 6, 1942.

———. "Seaboard Winter Trains Are Beginning Their Runs." November 27, 1936.

———. "Services of American Women Needed." March 17, 1944.

———. "Smithsonian Institute Making Explorations at Indian Mound." March 7, 1930.

———. "Tampa Man Killed as Train Hits Meat Truck at Seaboard Crossing." September 4, 1953.

———. "Three Have Narrow Escape." January 3, 1930.

———. "Tom Palmer, Noted Lawyer, Dies." August 16, 1946.

———. "The Truth about Safety Harbor." February 5, 1926.

———. "Two Orange Blossom Specials from Florida This Season." Advertisement, December 11 and 25, 1936.

———. "United States Involved in Worst War World Has Ever Known." December 12, 1941.

———. "U.S. Marine Aux. May Train at Safety Harbor." January 22, 1943.

Safety Harbor Resort and Spa. "Meetings & Conferences." http://www.safetyharborspa.com/meetconf (accessed August 16, 2013).

———. "Resort History." http://www.safetyharborspa.com/history/history.html (accessed August 16, 2013).

————. "Weddings & Special Occasions." http://www.safetyharborspa. com/wedoccasions (accessed August 16, 2013).

St. Petersburg Times. "Boxer Breland Likes Training Environs of Safety Harbor." September 2, 1986.

————. "Constable Wins Award for Arresting Robber." September 6, 1962.

————. "Experienced Man New Police Chief at Safety Harbor." December 29, 1946.

————. "Full Schedule Begins as New Train Arrives." January 4, 1929.

————. "Gomez Agrees to Terms With New York Team." March 3, 1935.

————. "Klan, Anti-Ike Propaganda at Safety Harbor Rally." May 2, 1952.

————. "Know Your Candidates for Constables." April 16, 1948.

————. "Mayor's Recall Rumored as Safety Harbor Acts to Restore Police Chief." April 18, 1957.

————. "NAACP Chief Throws a Barb." February 11, 1970.

————. "Nizer Backs LBJ's Policy on Vietnam." January 9, 1968.

————. "A Policy Before People." March 30, 1970.

————. "Political Battle Page." September 21, 1948.

————. "Police Department Abolition is Urged." October 22, 1971.

————. "Rigsby Seeks Re-election to Dist. 3 Constable Post." March 7, 1964.

————. "Robinson to Address Tampa NAACP Branch." February 25, 1966.

————. "Roll of Honor." October 27, 1918.

————. "Safety Harbor Board Discusses New Policeman." February 17, 1954.

————. "Safety Harbor Chief Reports Much Activity." January 16, 1963.

————. "Safety Harbor Chief Resigns." May 2, 1957.

————. "Safety Harbor Chief to Quit Monday." October 15, 1950.

————. "Safety Harbor Chief to Seek Constable Post." February 2, 1960.

————. "Safety Harbor Delays Decision on Police Issue." June 25, 1975.

————. "Safety Harbor Employs Paid Fire Captain." October 3, 1973.

————. "Safety Harbor Fires 2 Officials at Stormy Session." June 18, 1957.

————. "Safety Harbor Officials Fuss over Police Rule." April 2, 1957.

————. "Safety Harbor Officials Told Not to Shame City." April 17, 1957.

————. "Safety Harbor Police Chief Gets Telephone." August 8, 1957.

————. "Safety Harbor Police Department Now Legal." March 8, 1960.

————. "Safety Harbor Police Force Adds Patrolman." January 5, 1955.

————. "Safety Harbor Police Force Has 7-Man Auxiliary Unit." May 1, 1969.

————. "Safety Harbor Policeman Resigns Job." March 15, 1957.

————. "Safety Harbor Prohibits Open Fires." June 29, 1979.

————. "Safety Harbor Spa Improved." January 17, 1937.

————. "Safety Harbor Spa Robbery Loss Mounts." March 4, 1959.

————. "Safety Harbor: The Train Rumbles Through." December 1, 1965.

————. "Safety Harbor Tries Again; Names 3rd Chief." March 2, 1957.

———. "Safety Harbor Votes to Allow Abolition of Police Department." June 9, 1976.

———. "Safety Harbor Votes to Keep Police Force." July 9, 1975.

———. "SAL to Expand Train Service." November 5, 1946.

———. "Southbound Freight Kills Young Truck Driver." September 3, 1953.

———. "They Live in Brooklyn." March 30, 1970.

———. "Train Greeted By Band Here on First Trip." January 4, 1934.

———. "Two File in Safety Harbor Mayor Race." October 9, 1962.

———. "Two Injured at Shooting at Tavern." June 14, 1971.

———. "2 Offices in County Have No Candidates." May 22, 1932.

Schell, Rolfe F. *De Soto Didn't Land at Tampa*. Ft. Myers Beach, FL: Island Press, 1966.

Schnur, James A. "From Punta Pinal to Peerless Pinellas." Remarks delivered at the Inaugural "Pinellas by the Decades" Program, Heritage Village, September 11, 2011.

———. *Historic Pinellas County, A Centennial History*. San Antonio, TX: HPNbooks, 2012.

———. *Heritage Villagers: A Social History of the Pinellas Peninsula as Revealed through the Structures at Heritage Village*. Published by the author, 2004. Available online at http://dspace.nelson.usf.edu/xmlui/handle/10806/138.

Schultz, David. "Constables Resist Claim Their Jobs Unnecessary." *Evening Independent*, September 21, 1964.

Shaer, Matthew. "Ponce De Leon Never Searched for the Fountain of Youth." *Smithsonian Magazine*, June 2013. Available online at http://www.smithsonianmag.com/history-archaeology/Ponce-De-Leon-Never-Searched-for-the-Fountain-of-Youth-208345831.html.

Smith, Buckingham, trans., and David O. True, ed. *Memoir of Do. d'Escalante Fontaneda Respecting Florida*. Coral Gables, FL: Glades House, 1945. [Reprint of the Miami: University of Miami and the Historical Association of Southern Florida, 1944 edition.]

Starkey, Jay. *Things I Remember, 1899–1979*. Brooksville: Southwest Florida Water Management District, 1980.

Steffens, Judi Baker. E-mail message to the authors, May 5, 2013.

Stirling, Matthew W. "Mounds of the Vanished Calusa Indians of Florida," *Explorations and Fieldwork of the Smithsonian Institution in 1930*. Washington, D.C.: Smithsonian Institution, 1931.

Straight, William M. "Odet Philippe: Friend of Napoleon, Naval Surgeon and Pinellas Pioneer." *Journal of the Florida Medical Association* 53, no. 8 (August 1966): 704–10.

Straub, W.L. *History of Pinellas County, Florida*. St. Augustine, FL: Record Company, 1929.

Stevenson, Arielle. "Farewell to the Citrus King: Remembering Orange Blossom Groves' Al Repetto." *Creative Loafing*, July 20, 2012.

Swanton, John R. "De Soto's First Headquarters in Florida," *Florida Historical Quarterly* 30, no. 4 (April 1952): 311–16.

———. *Final Report of the United States De Soto Expedition Commission*, 1938. Reprint with introduction by Jeffrey Brain. Washington, D.C.: Smithsonian Institution Press, 1985.

Thompson, Tom. "Rigsby Retires." *Evening Independent*, February 10, 1981.

Tropical Breeze Publications. *Safety Harbor Museum of Regional History, Pioneers of Safety Harbor*. Safety Harbor, FL: Tropical Breeze Publications, 1998.

U.S. Patent and Trademark Office Full Text and Image Database. www.uspto.gov.

Walker, Meg. "Safety Harbor Faces Repairs on its Pier." *Evening Independent*, September 24, 1985.

Weber, David J. *The Spanish Frontier in North America*. New Haven, CT: Yale University Press, 1992.

Weddle, Robert S. "Early Spanish Exploration: The Caribbean, Central America, and the Gulf of Mexico." In *North American Exploration*. Vol. 1, *A New World Disclosed*, edited by John Logan Allen, pp. 189–240. Lincoln: University of Nebraska Press, 1997.

———. "Soto's Problems of Orientation: Maps, Navigation, and Instruments in the Florida Expedition." In *The Hernando de Soto Expedition*, edited by Patricia Galloway. Lincoln: University of Nebraska Press, 1997.

Weekly Challenger. "Bill Blackshear: One of the Cornerstones of the Weekly Challenger." September 7, 2011.

Willey, Gordon R. *Archeology of the Florida Gulf Coast*. Gainesville: University Press of Florida, 1998, orig. published 1949.

Worth, John E. "Fontaneda Revisited: Five Descriptions of Sixteenth-Century Florida." *Florida Historical Quarterly* 73, no. 3 (January 1995): 339–52.

———. "A History of Southeastern Indians in Cuba, 1513–1823." Paper presented at the 61st Annual Meeting of the Southeastern Archaeological Conference, St. Louis, Missouri, October 21–23, 2004.

———. "The Pineland Site and Calusa-Spanish Relations, 1612–1614." *Friends of the Randell Research Center* 4, no. 2 (June 2005). Available online at http://www.flmnh.ufl.edu/rrc/RRC_Vol4_No2.pdf.

Zinsser, L.H. "Letter to the Holders of Bonds of the City of Safety Harbor, Florida." January 1936. On file in archives at the Safety Harbor Museum and Cultural Center.

INDEX

A

Abbey, Sylvan (girl) 12, 73
Alden apartment building
　103, 140
Alligator Creek 51, 75,
　141, 153
　Alligator Lake 142, 163
Anderson, Police Chief
　John 144, 145, 151
Armed Occupation Act of
　1842 12, 59, 68,
　71, 76
Art Park 164

B

Bailey, Colonel William
　12, 70, 79, 80
Baker, Judi 67, 126
bankruptcy 13, 107, 120,
　134, 147
Banks, Goldie 86, 87,
　127, 128
Baranoff, Dr. Salem 14, 83,
　114, 115, 116, 117,
　118, 120, 146, 159
　ghost of 120

Baranoff Oak 164, 165
Baranoff Park 164
Barth, Dr. Con F. 13, 111
baseball 108, 123, 163
Bayshore Hotel 93
Bayshore Linear
　Greenway
　Recreational
　Trail 163
Bayview, Florida 70, 72,
　89, 95, 121, 149
Benson, Police Chief
　Howard E. 151
Bilgore Canning
　Company 65
Blackshear, William 14,
　65, 125, 132, 133,
　134, 142
　election of 133
Bonaparte, Napoleon 57,
　58, 59, 62
Booth, Odet W.
　"Keeter" 12, 69,
　70, 109, 144
Booth, Richard 12, 69,
　71, 73, 159
boxing 109, 112, 120, 144

Boyd, E.A. 91
Brasfield, Sandie 67, 118
Bristow, James 64
Brooklyn Heights 93, 124,
　134, 135, 136, 137
　lack of services 134, 136
Bullen, Ripley 14, 42, 51

C

Cabeza de Vaca, Alvar
　Nunez 24
Cahow, Daisy 13, 158
Calusa 11, 33, 34, 35, 36,
　37, 38, 42, 47
Calusa-Tocobaga Peace
　Treaty 33, 36, 37,
　38, 43
Campbell, G.W. 99
Cancer de Barbastro, Fray
　Luis 11, 28, 29,
　30, 31, 32, 35, 37
　contact with the
　Tocobaga 30
　death of 31
Carlos (Calusa chief) 34,
　35, 36, 37, 38

Carroll, Thora 150
cemeteries
  African American 131,
    132
  McMullen 73
  Sylvan Abbey 73, 74,
    131, 156
Chalk Festival 167
Chamber of Commerce
  147, 165
Charlotte Harbor 25, 33
cigars 55, 58, 60, 62
citrus 15, 55, 58, 59, 60,
    62, 63, 64, 65, 67,
    72, 88, 91, 121,
    123, 126, 128
city hall 145, 150, 156,
    165, 167
citywide emergency
    144, 151
Civil War 12, 61, 70, 72,
    76, 77, 80
Clearwater, Florida (Clear
    Water) 12, 16, 67,
    91, 92, 94, 99, 105,
    109, 110, 117, 123,
    125, 128, 131, 133,
    136, 137, 149, 158
Cooley, William 68
Courtney Campbell
    Causeway 13, 16,
    69, 70, 100, 105
Curie, Marie and
    Pierre 84

D

Daisy Douglas Park 163
Dalwig, John Conrad 79
Davis Causeway.
    See Courtney
    Campbell
    Causeway
De Leon, Ponce 21, 27,
    33, 84
Dennis, Caryl 165

Dent, Laura 146
Denton, Earl 110
De Soto, Hernando 11,
    16, 21, 22, 23,
    24, 25, 26, 28,
    29, 30, 31, 32,
    42, 43, 45, 79,
    83, 84, 160, 168
  possible site of first
    encampment 25,
    26, 31, 43, 79
  route of expedition 25
Devnani, Salu 119
Downs, Mayor Ben 14,
    109, 144, 145
  recall election 14, 145
  telephone usage 145
Dr. Barth's Hotel & Baths
    13, 82, 111

E

"elf tree" 52
Espiritu Santo Catholic
    Church 28
Espiritu Santo Springs 12,
    13, 14, 21, 70, 78,
    79, 80, 82, 84, 86,
    87, 102, 107, 111,
    112, 114, 160
  1910 pamphlet 84, 86
  restorative properties
    80, 83, 84, 86,
    87, 101
  taste of 83

F

fire
  1917 blaze 13, 99,
    100, 165
  at pier 148
  Bayshore Hotel 93
  in community 101, 107,
    131, 155
  McMullen log cabin 71

fire department 13, 91,
    99, 100, 149, 150,
    151, 153, 154, 155,
    156, 157
  volunteer force 138
Florida land boom 104
  end of 105, 112
Florida State Museum 51
Fontaneda, Hernando de
    Escalante 42, 46
Fort Brooke 59, 60, 69, 79
Fountain of Youth 16,
    21, 22, 27, 84,
    87, 160, 166

G

Ganley, Gladys 18, 62, 70,
    88, 89, 93, 95
Gomez, John 58, 59, 60
grapefruit 55, 60, 62, 63,
    64, 67, 118, 128
Green Cove Springs,
    Florida 89, 96
Green, Dr. J.T. 80, 84
Green, Jesse D. 80, 83
Green Springs 12, 80, 88,
    89, 91, 96, 99, 121
Green Springs Inn 91, 99
Griffin, John 14, 51
Gubner, Dr. Richard
    117, 119

H

Hankins Hotel 91
Harbor Bar 143
Harborside Studios 165
Harrington, Cecil 140
haunted places
  house belonging to
    settler 89
  spa 120
  St. Frances Hotel 165
Hedgeman, Yvonne 131
Heritage Village 71,
    91, 185

house numbers, lack of 127
hunting 40, 76, 108, 142
hurricanes
    1848 12, 49, 60, 61,
        71, 102
    1921 13, 102, 103
    Elena (1985) 14, 148
    Gladys (1968) 156

I

Ingersoll, Mary 140

J

Jacobsen Trailer Plant
    146
Jansik, Dr. Alben 13, 113,
    114, 115
John Wilson Park 148,
    162, 163, 165

K

Kapok Tree Inn 126
Kothe, Lisa 159
Ku Klux Klan 129, 130

L

Largo, Florida 64, 71, 73,
    89, 121, 123, 149
Lawton, Carl W. 94,
    95, 140
Lawton-Harrington
    American Legion
    Post 140, 146
Lehman, B.J. 141, 165
library 13, 14, 18, 52, 103,
    105, 144, 146, 158,
    159, 164, 167, 168
Lincoln Highlands 103,
    132, 133, 134,
    136, 137
Lover's Oak tree 12, 51,
    52, 95, 109
Lutz, Charles 122, 123

M

Magdalena 30, 31, 32
    deception by 30, 31, 32
Marshall Street Park 163
Mattie Williams
    Neighborhood
    Family Center 137
Mayor's Court 150
McMullen, Captain James
    P. "Captain Jim"
    12, 63, 68, 70, 71,
    72, 73, 74, 88, 102,
    156
McMullen, Ward 102, 141
Mease Park 163
Meat frenzy 125
Menendez de Aviles,
    Pedro 11, 33, 34,
    35, 36, 37, 38, 41,
    42, 43, 47, 48, 147
Milanich, Professor Jerald
    26, 36, 42
Miller, Jim 147
mineral springs 15, 21,
    60, 79, 80, 83, 84,
    91, 101, 105, 111,
    113, 115, 123, 168
Mocoso 26, 41, 43, 45
Morrow, Bobby 150, 155
Mounds, Tocobaga 12,
    26, 31, 32, 39, 45,
    46, 48, 49, 50, 51,
    60, 71, 132, 164
    destruction of 26, 52, 71
    Lover's Oak 51, 52
    Pipkin 51, 52, 164
Mullet Creek Park 162
Munoz, Juan 30, 31, 32
Myrick, Luella 136, 137

N

Narvaez, Panfilo de 11,
    23, 24, 26, 28, 29,
    30, 31, 46

rescue party 24, 26
natural springs. *See*
    mineral springs
Nelson, William 68, 69
newspapers
    Safety Harbor Herald 13,
        94, 102, 128, 129,
        138, 146, 165
    Tropical Breeze 13, 62, 94,
        165
Nichols, David 117, 118,
    125, 140
Nolte, Valerie 126
North City Park 163

O

Oldsmar, Florida 13, 103,
    109, 117, 123, 142,
    149, 156
Olympia Development
    Group 14, 120
Ortiz, Juan 24, 26, 45, 46

P

Palmer, Thomas 14, 49,
    51, 143
Pearce, Louise 73, 124
Petree, Glenn O. 126
Philippe, Odet 12, 15, 49,
    55, 56, 57, 58, 59,
    60, 61, 62, 63, 64,
    67, 68, 69, 70, 72,
    77, 79, 94, 164
Philippe Park 11, 12, 13,
    14, 25, 26, 30, 32,
    37, 41, 47, 51, 55,
    62, 67, 125, 132,
    134, 143, 164
pilleau, chicken 95, 141
pioneers
    conditions faced by 75
    furniture 75
    home construction 75
    hunting 76

population growth in
    region 77
travel to Tampa 76
Pipkin, Daniel M. 52, 82,
    165
Pipkin Mineral Wells 82,
    112
pirates 58, 59, 60
Players of Safety Harbor
    (P.O.S.H.) 167
Poetry Festival 168
Pojoy 41
police department 144,
    145, 147, 149, 150,
    151, 153
  abolition of 153
post office 12, 72, 76, 88,
    96, 100, 107, 139,
    141
  dispatch desk 159
Purvis, Christine 141

R

radioactivity 84, 86
rail 12, 13, 64, 65, 75,
    89, 94, 110, 112,
    120, 121, 123,
    124, 125, 126,
    127, 128, 136, 147
  accidents 124, 125, 126
  boxcars used as homes
    124
  Orange Belt Railway
    121, 123
  Orange Blossom Special
    123
  Seaboard Air Line
    Railway 82, 123,
    124, 128, 136
  Tampa & Gulf Coast
    Railway 123
Ramquist, Todd and
    Kiaralinda 166
Rigsby, Claude 110, 130,
    148, 152, 153, 162

arrest of Gordon
    Abel 153
Rigsby, Clyde 110, 130
Rigsby Recreation
    Center 162
Rogel, Father Juan de 37,
    38, 42
Rountree, Bertha 165

S

Safety Harbor Art and
    Music Center 14,
    130, 166
Safety Harbor City
    Park 163
Safety Harbor culture
    41, 43
Safety Harbor Garden
    Club 162
Safety Harbor Incised
    pottery 50
Safety Harbor Museum
    and Cultural
    Center 52, 93,
    107, 147, 150, 159,
    162, 166, 167
Safety Harbor Public Art
    Committee 167
Safety Harbor Senior
    Living 165
Samnik, Joe 143
schoolhouse
  Lincoln Heights 139,
    157, 158
  McMullen log cabin 73
  Safety Harbor Junior
    High 157
  Safety Harbor School
    13, 94, 157
  Sylvan Abbey 73, 88,
    124
Seafood Festival 148
Second Seminole War 58,
    59, 68, 74, 79

Seminole people, contact
    with 74
Shower, A.E. 13, 18,
    94, 102, 138,
    146, 155, 159
Shower, Franklin 155
Silver Dome Apartments
    104, 147
smallpox 13, 38, 129,
    130, 150
Smallwood, Frank 94
Smithsonian Institution
    13, 49, 50, 51
spa 14, 15, 21, 22, 102,
    103, 109, 111, 114,
    116, 117, 118, 119,
    120, 142, 145, 146,
    159, 160, 164
  robbery of 145
  "ten commandments"
    116
Spanish artifacts 13, 14,
    25, 37, 48, 50, 51
Spanish flu 101
Spencer, Lois 148
St. Augustine 33
St. Frances Hotel 100,
    165
Stirling, Dr. Matthew W.
    13, 49, 50
St. James Hotel 13, 103,
    111, 113, 114, 116,
    165
Straub, W.L. 25, 64, 75,
    96
Sun Grove shop 67
Sunshine Park racetrack
    142
Syd Entel Galleries and
    Susan Benjamin
    Glass 166
Sylvan Abbey Methodist
    Church 73, 88, 91

T

Tampa Bay Musicians'
    Co-op 167
Tavern, the 143
Third Friday Music Series
    160, 162, 163
Thomas, George B. 91
Tilmann, Ian 163
Tocobaga 11, 13, 14, 15,
    26, 30, 31, 32, 33,
    35, 36, 37, 38, 39,
    40, 41, 42, 43, 45,
    46, 47, 48, 50, 51,
    78, 143, 147
  burial customs 46
  clothing 45
  diet 43
  end of 39, 47
  excavations 8, 14, 25,
    42, 46, 47, 48, 49,
    50, 51
  hunting by 43
  pottery 13, 14, 46, 47,
    50, 51
  settlement near
    Tallahassee 47
  society of 41, 42, 43,
    45, 46, 47
  village 11, 15, 25, 26,
    31, 36, 37, 38, 43,
    45, 46, 47, 48, 50,
    51, 79
treaty between the Safety
    Harbor Museum
    and the United
    Lenape Band 147
Tucker, James and Virginia
    12, 78, 80, 82, 84,
    86, 101, 103, 111,
    112, 113, 165

U

Ucita 21, 24, 25, 26, 27,
    41, 42, 45, 46

V

Vasbinder, Constable Percy
    150, 151, 152
Veterans Memorial
    Park 162
Voting Rights Act 133

W

Waldron, A.G. 94
Walton, Captain John
    37, 47
Washington, Captain
    George 88
Washington, C.S. 88
Whimzey House 166
Whitehead, Dolly
    Brader 118
Williams, Mattie 137
Women's Civic Club
    108, 158
Works Progress
    Administration
    13, 105, 158
World War I 94, 140, 150
World War II 114, 138,
    140

Y

Youngblood, Sid 12, 89,
    99, 159

Z

Zinsser, Mayor Louis 105,
    106, 138

ABOUT THE AUTHORS

LAURA KEPNER is a full-time writer. Her love of history and the people who contributed to it are the inspirations behind much of her work. Laura is an avid reader, volunteer and part-time creative writing instructor. She lives in Safety Harbor with her husband, Chris, and the two youngest of their four adult children.

An aspiring novelist and avid book collector, **WARREN FIRSCHEIN** is a longtime attorney for a federal regulatory agency. He is a graduate of the University of Pittsburgh School of Law and also holds a degree in political science from the University of Rochester and an MBA from Carnegie-Mellon University. Warren was recently named a finalist of the Norma Crosier 91-Word Memoir contest and is currently finishing his first novel for middle-grade students. He lives in Safety Harbor, Florida, with his wife, Dawn, and two daughters, Sophie and Elena.

www.ingramcontent.com/pod-product-compliance
Lightning Source LLC
Chambersburg PA
CBHW060758100426

42813CB00004B/861